MULTICU

JAMES A. BANKS, ~

(continued)

Multicultural Strategies for Education and Social Change:
Carriers of the Torch in the United States
and South Africa
ARNETHA F. BALL

We Can't Teach What We Don't Know:
White Teachers, Multiracial Schools, Second Edition
GARY R. HOWARD

Un-Standardizing Curriculum: Multicultural Teaching in
the Standards-Based Classroom
CHRISTINE E. SLEETER

Beyond the Big House:
African American Educators on Teacher Education
GLORIA LADSON-BILLINGS

Teaching and Learning in Two Languages:
Bilingualism and Schooling in the United States
EUGENE E. GARCÍA

Improving Multicultural Education:
Lessons from the Intergroup Education Movement
CHERRY A. McGEE BANKS

Education Programs for Improving Intergroup Relations:
Theory, Research, and Practice
WALTER G. STEPHAN AND W. PAUL VOGT, EDS.

Walking the Road:
Race, Diversity, and Social Justice in Teacher Education
MARILYN COCHRAN-SMITH

City Schools and the American Dream:
Reclaiming the Promise of Public Education
PEDRO A. NOGUERA

Thriving in the Multicultural Classroom:
Principles and Practices for Effective Teaching
MARY DILG

Educating Teachers for Diversity: Seeing with a Cultural Eye
JACQUELINE JORDAN IRVINE

Teaching Democracy:
Unity and Diversity in Public Life
WALTER C. PARKER

The Making—and Remaking—of a Multiculturalist
CARLOS E. CORTÉS

Transforming the Multicultural Education
of Teachers: Theory, Research, and Practice
MICHAEL VAVRUS

Learning to Teach for Social Justice
LINDA DARLING-HAMMOND, JENNIFER FRENCH, AND
SILVIA PALOMA GARCIA-LOPEZ, EDS.

Culture, Difference, and Power
CHRISTINE E. SLEETER

Learning and Not Learning English:
Latino Students in American Schools
GUADALUPE VALDÉS

The Children Are Watching:
How the Media Teach About Diversity
CARLOS E. CORTÉS

Race and Culture in the Classroom:
Teaching and Learning Through Multicultural Education
MARY DILG

Reducing Prejudice and Stereotyping in Schools
WALTER STEPHAN

Multicultural Education, Transformative Knowledge,
and Action: Historical and Contemporary Perspectives
JAMES A. BANKS, ED.

Class Rules

EXPOSING INEQUALITY
IN AMERICAN HIGH SCHOOLS

Peter W. Cookson Jr.

Teachers College
Columbia University
New York and London

KH

Published by Teachers College Press, 1234 Amsterdam Avenue,
New York, NY 10027

Library of Congress Cataloging-in-Publication Data

Cookson, Peter W.
   Class rules : exposing inequality in American high schools /
Peter W. Cookson Jr.
      pages cm. — (Multicultural education series)
   Includes bibliographical references and index.
   ISBN 978-0-8077-5452-8 (pbk. : alk. paper)
   ISBN 978-0-8077-5453-5 (hardcover : alk. paper)
   1. Educational sociology—United States. 2. Children with social
disabilities—Education—United States. 3. Discrimination in education—
United States. 4. Multicultural education—United States. I. Title.
   LC191.4.C67 2013
   306.43'2–dc23   2013015703

ISBN 978-0-8077-5452-8 (paperback)
ISBN 978-0-8077-5453-5 (hardcover)

Printed on acid-free paper
Manufactured in the United States of America

20 19 18 17 16 15 14 13   8 7 6 5 4 3 2 1

10/6/14

Contents

Series Foreword

This interesting, informative, and engaging book reveals how class shapes the educational experiences of students by describing the institutional cultures of five high schools that have contrasting social-class characteristics. Cookson adapts and uses Lightfoot's (1983) observational lens of portraiture to describe them. One is an elite boarding school. The others are public schools located in four different types of communities: (1) a wealthy suburb; (2) a middle-class neighborhood; (3) a working-class rural community; (4) and a low-income urban community. Cookson describes how the structure, rites of passage, and "class consciousness" in each school reproduce social-class inequality.

Cookson's book is within the tradition of a group of important and influential studies completed since the early 1970s that examine the effects of social class on education. Some of the most compelling and contested of these books were written by revisionist scholars who challenged the notion that the American common school is the "great equalizer" as envisioned by Horace Mann, the "father of American education," and as described by educational historians such as Cremin (1965) and Ravitch (1978). Greer (1972) wrote one of the most searing critiques of schools as the "great equalizer," which he dismissively referred to as "the great school legend." Bowles and Gintis (1976) support Greer's analysis by maintaining that schools, rather than promoting social-class equality, socialize students to function effectively within the structure of the workplace. Jencks and his colleagues, in their widely discussed and contested 1972 book, *Inequality: A Reassessment of the Effect of Family and Schooling in America*, argue that family background has a more powerful effect on student cognitive outcomes than do schools. A more recent book by Anyon (1997), *Ghetto Schooling: A Political Economy of Urban Educational Reform*, describes how class and the political economy structure limit the ability of schools to actualize social-class equality.

Cookson's book is a timely and significant addition to the genre of work that examines the effects of social class on education because of recent developments in the United States related to class and inequality. These trends include the growing social-class gap in U.S. society, the extensive public attention that this gap has received since the financial crisis of 2007–2008, and the Occupy Wall Street movement which began in 2011 in New York City's Zuccotti Park against social and economic inequality. A number of recent and notable books describe the wide economic and social-class gap in the United States, including Murray's (2012) *Coming Apart: The State of White America, 1960–2010*, and Stiglitz's (2012) *The Price of Inequality: How Today's Divided Society Endangers Our Future*. Stiglitz points out that between 2002 and 2007, the top 1 percent of the U.S. population acquired more than 65 percent of the growth in national income.

Cookson's book can help researchers, policymakers, and practicing educators to seriously ponder and grapple with the powerful ways in which social-class inequality shapes the culture and structure of schools. This kind of reflection will help policymakers and administrators to make more complex analyses of the causes of the academic achievement gap, to better understand the ways in which the political economic structures and limits the role of teachers and students, and to formulate creative ways to educate the diverse students that increasingly populate the nation's schools.

American classrooms are experiencing the largest influx of immigrant students since the beginning of the 20th century. Almost 14 million new immigrants—documented and undocumented—settled in the United States in the years from 2000 to 2010. Less than 10% came from nations in Europe. Most came from Mexico, nations in Asia, and nations in Latin America, the Caribbean, and Central America (Camarota, 2011). A large but undetermined number of undocumented immigrants enter the United States each year. The U.S. Department of Homeland Security (2010) estimated that in January 2010 10.8 million undocumented immigrants were living in the United States, a decrease from the estimated 11.8 million in January 2007, among which were approximately 3.2 million children and young adults, most of whom grew up in this country (Perez, 2011). The influence of an increasingly ethnically diverse population on U.S. schools, colleges, and universities is and will continue to be enormous.

Schools in the United States are more diverse today than they have been since the early 1900s when a multitude of immigrants entered the United States from Southern, Central, and Eastern Europe. In the 20-year period between 1989 and 2009, the percentage of students of color in U.S. public schools increased from 32% to 45% (Aud, Hussar, Kena, Bianco, Frohlich, Kemp, & Tahan, 2011). If current trends continue, students of color will equal or exceed the percentage of White students in U.S. public schools within one or two decades. In 2010–2011, students of color exceeded the number of White students in the District of Columbia and in 13 states (listed in descending order of the percentage of ethnic minority students therein): Hawaii, California, New Mexico, Texas, Nevada, Arizona, Florida,

Maryland, Mississippi, Georgia, Louisiana, Delaware, and New York (Aud, Hussar, Johnson, Kena, Roth, Manning, Wang, & Zhang, 2012). In 2009, children of undocumented immigrants made up 6.8% of students in grades kindergarten through 12 (Perez, 2011).

Language and religious diversity is also increasing in the U.S. student population. The 2010 American Community Survey indicates that approximately 19.8% of the school-age population spoke a language at home other than English in 2010 (U.S. Census Bureau, 2010). The Progressive Policy Institute (2008) estimated that 50 million Americans (out of 300 million) spoke a language at home other than English in 2008. Harvard professor Diana L. Eck (2001) calls the United States the "most religiously diverse nation on earth" (p. 4). Islam is now the fastest-growing religion in the United State, as well as in several European nations such as France, the United Kingdom, and The Netherlands (Banks, 2009; Cesari, 2004). Most teachers now in the classroom and in teacher education programs are likely to have students from diverse ethnic, racial, linguistic, and religious groups in their classrooms during their careers. This is true for both inner-city and suburban teachers in the United States, as well as those in many other Western nations such as Canada, Australia, and the United Kingdom (Banks, 2009).

The major purpose of the Multicultural Education Series is to provide preservice educators, practicing educators, graduate students, scholars, and policymakers with an interrelated and comprehensive set of books that summarizes and analyzes important research, theory, and practice related to the education of ethnic, racial, cultural, and linguistic groups in the United States and the education of mainstream students about diversity. The dimensions of multicultural education, developed by Banks (2004) and described in the *Handbook of Research on Multicultural Education* and in the *Encyclopedia of Diversity in Education* (Banks, 2012), provide the conceptual framework for the development of the publications in the Series. They are content integration, the knowledge construction process, prejudice reduction, an equity pedagogy, and an empowering institutional culture and social structure.

The books in the Series provide research, theoretical, and practical knowledge about the behaviors and learning characteristics of students of color, language minority students, and low-income students. They also provide knowledge about ways to improve academic achievement and race relations in educational settings. Multicultural education is consequently as important for middle-class White suburban students as it is for students of color who live in the inner city. Multicultural education fosters the public good and the overarching goals of the commonwealth.

Unlike the revisionist critiques of schooling that were published in the 1970s whose authors had little faith in the potential for public schools to make a difference in the lives of students, Cookson believes that schools can and should be a powerful factor in determining the life chances of students. He describes actions that educators and policymakers can take to change the class-based school system in the United States. To achieve this goal, restructuring at a deep level is essential and educational policy must have a social and ethical framework that is grounded in "civic values and faith in ourselves." Other modifications are essential, including changing the way public education is funded, altering the curriculum so that it helps all students to acquire shared collective memories of the United States, placing education into the hands of teachers and other educators, and curtailing the testing that is pervasive and pernicious within the schools. Cookson's ideas for school reform that will reduce the powerful effects of social-class inequality merit serious consideration and reflection by policymakers and educational practitioners.

James A. Banks

REFERENCES

Anyon, J. (1997). *Ghetto schooling: A political economy of urban educational reform*. New York: Teachers College Press.

Aud, S., Hussar, W., Johnson, F., Kena, G., Roth, E., Manning, E., Wang, X., & Zhang, J. (2012). *The condition of education 2012* (NCES 2012-045). Washington, DC: U.S. Department of Education, National Center for Education Statistics. Retrieved from http://nces.ed.gov/pubsearch

Aud, S., Hussar, W., Kena, G., Bianco, K., Frohlich, L., Kemp, J., & Tahan, K. (2011). *The condition of education 2011* (NCES 2011-033). U.S. Department of Education, National Center for Education Statistics. Washington, DC: U.S. Department of Education, National Center for Education Statistics. Retrieved from http://nces.ed.gov/programs/coe/pdf/coe_1er.pdf

Banks, J. A. (2004). Multicultural education: Historical development, dimensions, and practice. In J. A. Banks & C. A. M. Banks (Eds.), *Handbook of research on multicultural education* (2nd ed., pp. 3–29). San Francisco: Jossey-Bass.

Banks, J. A. (Ed.). (2009). *The Routledge international companion to multicultural education*. New York and London: Routledge.

Banks, J. A. (2012). Multicultural education: Dimensions of. In J. A. Banks (Ed.), *Encyclopedia of diversity in education* (vol. 3, pp. 1538–1547). Thousand Oaks, CA: Sage Publications.

Bowles, S., & Gintis, H. (1976). *Schooling in capitalist America: Educational reform and the contradictions of economic life*. New York: Basic Books.

Camarota, S. A. (2011, October). *A record-setting decade of immigration: 2000 to 2010*. Washintgton, DC: Center for Immigration Studies. Retrieved from http://cis.org/2000-2010-record-setting-decade-of-immigration

Cesari, J. (2004). *When Islam and democracy meet: Muslims in Europe and the United States.* New York: Pelgrave Macmillan.

Cremin, L. A. (1965). *The genius of American education.* New York: Vintage Books.

Eck, D. L. (2001). *A new religious America: How a "Christian country" has become the world's most religiously diverse nation.* New York: HarperSanFrancisco.

Greer, C. (1972). *The great school legend: A revisionist interpretation of American public education.* New York: Basic Books.

Jencks, C., Smith, M., Aciand, H., Bane, M. J., Cohen, D., et al. (1972). *Inequality: A reassessment of the effect of family and schooling in America.* New York: Basic Books.

Lightfoot, S. L. (1983). *The good high school: Portraits of character and culture.* New York: Basic Books.

Murray, C. (2012). *Coming apart: The state of White America, 1960–2010.* New York: Crown Forum.

Perez, W. (2011). *Americans by heart: Undocumented Latino students and the promise of higher education.* New York: Teachers College Press.

Progressive Policy Institute. (2008). *50 million Americans speak languages other than English at home.* Retrieved from http://www.ppionline.org/ppi_ci.cfm?knlgAreaID=108&subsecID=900003&contentID=254619

Ravitch, D. (1978). *The revisionists revised: A critique of the racial attack on the schools.* New York: Basic Books.

Stiglitz, J. E. (2012). *The price of inequality: How today's divided society endangers our future.* New York: Norton.

U.S. Census Bureau. (2008, August 14). *Statistical abstract of the United States.* Retrieved from http://www.census.gov/prod/2006pubs/07statab/pop.pdf

U.S. Census Bureau. (2010). *2010 American community survey.* Retrieved from http://factfinder2.census.gov/faces/tableservices/jsf/pages/productview.xhtml?pid=ACS_10_1YR_S1603&prodType=table

U.S. Department of Homeland Security. (2010, February). *Estimates of the unauthorized immigrant population residing in the United States: January 2010.* Retrieved from http://www.dhs.gov/files/statistics/immigration.shtm

Class Rules

Introduction

Socialization . . . goes all the way down.
—*Richard Rorty*

THE QUESTION

Class Rules is an exploration of one of education's most persistent questions: What is the role of schools in creating and maintaining class divisions? Answering this question is a complex conceptual and empirical puzzle—and controversial. Even raising the class question puts the equalitarian and meritocratic mission of education under the scholarly and policy microscope in a way that is sometimes threatening. To suggest that our most popular and enduring social myth—the leveling of the social and economic playing field through education—does not bear close scrutiny is to invite opposition.

Equality of educational opportunity is a cherished part of the American story of upward mobility and social justice. But the evidence that where and with whom a student goes to school significantly influences his or her life chances and lifestyles is substantial. One of the most important levers in turning the educational playing field into a geography of mountains and valleys is the class composition of schools' student bodies (Apple, 1995; Archer, 1979; Bigelow, 1992; Connell et al., 1982, 2012; Cookson, 1994; Fine, 1992; Floud, 1973; Golden, 2007; Goode, 1967; Halsey, Heath, & Ridge, 1980; Ornstein, 2007; Persell, 1977; Rehberg & Rosenthal, 1978; Rosenbaum, 1976; Rothenberg, 2000; Rothstein, 2004; Ryan, 2010; Sacks, 2007).

There are several ways this stratification of educational opportunities might operate: Schools might be socially neutral environments that have no or very little effect on students' class position and thus reproduce class differences by simply not disturbing existing class characteristics; schools might reinforce class position organizationally, passing on networking advantages to students; and last, schools, particularly high schools, might pass on class position through *rites of passage* that instill in students the values, dispositions, and beliefs of their class and, in doing so, solidify class divides and class consciousness. This in turn would allow for the "natural" reproduction of class positions.

Class Rules examines this last proposition. It is a sociological axiom that society precedes school. This is a fancy way of saying that schools reflect and shape the values of society. Most high schools are composed of students from very similar backgrounds due to wealth and race segregation and the existence of private-sector schools. But this fact alone does not mean that schools would be sequenced into a social dance where opportunities are allotted to students by class. It would take something else.

That something else is socialization. There are many ways in which young people are socialized; adolescents are socialized by their family, their neighborhoods, other students, and a myriad of factors that shape their social experience. Moreover, these experiences are filtered through socially constructed identities such as gender, race, and ethnicity. People are complex. But within this observation is another story that is seldom told. As different as we are, we are also similar in many ways—we tend to reflect the values, dispositions, and beliefs of the class into which we are born. Although class position is not the same as caste membership, it is a powerful definer of identity.

The founder of modern sociology, Emile Durkheim (Allan, 2010) captured this concept of how self and society merge when he suggested that the "totality of beliefs and sentiments common to the average members of society forms a determinate system with a life of its own. It can be termed the collective or common consciousness"(p. 108). More recently, British sociologist Margaret Archer (2000) reframed this observation into a problem: What is the relationship between social structure and human agency? How free are we really to establish our own individual identities especially if, in the words of philosopher Richard Rorty (1989), socialization goes all the way down?

MY ARGUMENT

The focus of *Class Rules* is not simply of academic interest; it speaks to a significant social problem. We ought to understand how class and schooling interact because social class is one of the most enduring dynamic engines of social stability, social change, and social control in modern industrial and postindustrial societies (Bourdieu, 1984; Bourdieu & Passeron, 1970; Bowles & Gintis, 1976; Femia, 1975; Giddens, 1973; Jencks et al., 1972; Lareau & Conley, 2008; Mills, 1956; Parenti, 1988; Parkin, 1971; Sennett & Cobb, 1972; Tumin, 1953; Wright, 2008). Race, gender, ethnicity, religion, and class all contribute to the narrative with which we write our conscious and unconscious autobiographies. In industrialized societies, however, class plays a leading role, if not the starring role, in the drama of social life (Baltzell, 1958, 1964; Birmingham, 1987; Brooks, 2000; Cookson & Persell, 1985; Douthat, 2005; Fussell, 1992; Gilbert, 2011; Lapham, 1988; Lenski, 1966).

In *Class Rules*, I unpack how high schools play a significant role in influencing our conscious and unconscious autobiographies and in doing so become social mechanisms for class reproduction. My project concentrates on the essential conceptual issues and gathers the relevant data. Put most simply, my argument is:

1. We know empirically that high schools are stratified by the class backgrounds of the students they serve; the higher the aggregate class background of a student body, the higher the social status of a school. There are two primary ways this stratification takes place: residential segregation and the existence of exclusive private-sector schools. We also have good reason to believe that high schools are socially sanctioned to produce graduates who are assigned to the class positions their schools have prepared them to assume (Meyer, 1970, 1977).

I hypothesize that there are two primary mechanisms by which this social sorting and selecting process takes place: credentialism (Collins, 1971, 1975, 1979) and the internalization of collective memory. Class-based educational credentials publicly certify class status rights. Class-based collective memories create bonds between class members, forming the basis of group identity that, when solidified, becomes class consciousness. I define school-based collective memory as the internalization of shared school experiences that remain active into adulthood. This concept is explored in depth in Chapter 1.

2. The development of collective memory is possible because the institutional life of schools is based on intense emotional interactions and relationships, which deeply affect adolescents' emerging identities. As author and scholar Howard Bloom (2000) has suggested, "memory is reality." It is our internal pool of recollections, reminiscences, and rationalizations from which we draw our understanding of who we are and where we belong. Elizabeth Loftus (1980), one of the world's most widely recognized memory researchers, conducted a series of experiments that demonstrated the power of group influence on memory. She showed a sample of college students a moving picture of a traffic accident and then measured how misinformation was passed on among the individuals based on erroneous reporting by influential members of the group. Minds are composed of many elements, including collective memories.

Using the analogy of a theatrical performance, I argue that the drama of schooling is composed of fictional narratives in which students, teachers, and administrators play roles in scripted and repetitive stories about who students are from a class perspective and their most likely class destinations. These are stories with social and emotional punch lines.

The creation of collective identities is forged when students undergo distinctive *class rites of passage*. A rite of passage is a ceremony marking a significant transition in a group's or individual's life. Rites of passage may be short or extended; for socialization purposes, extended rites of passage are most effective because they allow for repetition and permanent internalization. They also reduce resistance. I believe that when students pass through school-based class rites of passage, they internalize their school's class culture in real and lasting ways. I call this the deep curriculum of schooling.

3. In *Class Rules* this process of internalization is called *infusion* because the high school socialization experience is embracing and enduring. The infusion process creates shared memories of class solidarity, collective prejudices, and social attitudes. We are social animals; joining with other members of our species is one of our most basic survival strategies. In human societies we identify with our tribe, clan, caste, and class. Howard Bloom (2000) describes this tendency to pack among humans as follows:

> Experiments show that humans are drawn to those who share their attitudes on religion, politics, parents, drugs, music, ethnicity, and even clothes. They'll do everything from standing closer to their kindred-in-belief to marrying them in preference to someone other factors tag as a more likely candidate for matrimony. (p. 154)

Social scientist Meredith F. Small (1990) characterizes the social organization of primates in a way that implicitly underscores how group processes infuse us with our core identities:

> In contrast to schools of fishes or herds of ungulates, the primate groups are not mere aggregations but true social organizations, involving complicated interactions between members and usually maintaining long-term cohesiveness from generation to generation through a dynamic web of interpersonal intrigue. (p. 36)

We fear isolation because we require a group identity to have a clear sense of self. We become infused with the values, fantasies, prejudices, and dispositions of our primary social collective. The threat of exile is usually enough to ensure conformity. Although individualism is tolerated in marginal ways, it is institutionally limited by the fundamental organization of group life.

4. The primary research strategy utilized to uncover how high schools create their respective class rites of passage is comparative. By contrasting the institutional values, practices, and class assumptions of five representative high schools arrayed across the five major classes in the United States today, differing class rites of passage are systematically observed and compared. This comparative analysis allows us to examine how collective memory is institutionally created and transmitted across generations seamlessly and often permanently.

5. The implication of these findings is that until we develop a system of schools that limits the power of credentialing and creates trans-class collective memories there is little hope of achieving equality of educational opportunity.

It should be evident why I have called this study *Class Rules*. High schools enroll young, socially unformed adolescents and graduate adolescents who have been, in a social sense, reborn. From my perspective, the process of class reproduction plays a significant role in reproducing enduring inequality. Enduring inequalities are those that are passed from generation to generation. This passing on of social position can occur at many levels, including family, gender, race, ethnicity, religion, and nationality. I argue that although these forms of inequality are extremely important, the passage of class position from generation to generation is a key factor in shoring up structural inequality.

By definition, structural inequality is enduring, intergenerational, and insulated from cosmetic policy changes. To change structure a deep political change is needed. As Americans, we tend to think of inequality as a passing misfortune to be rectified by education or the result of individuals failing to work hard. But as we will see shortly, people who are born rich tend to die rich and people who are born poor tend to die poor—whether or not they work hard.

Because we are a society that believes in the power of individual effort, we are somewhat blinded by the structural processes that reproduce inequalities with regularity. Coming to terms with structural inequality requires a new way of thinking; it is my hope that *Class Rules* will help in a small way to shape a new way of thinking. We normally think of enduring inequality as being caused by macroeconomic factors in conjunction with politics—and these factors are hugely important. But a purely economic and political explanation of why social divisions persist leaves unexplained the role of human agency in creating and re-creating the social order. Without a social/psychological explanation of social reproduction, we are at risk of not seeing the social sinews that hold the skeleton of structural inequality in place.

To endure, inequality needs to be inscribed on the human heart as well as felt in the pocketbook. The acceptance of inequality is not an afterthought in the process of creating inequality; it is a precondition for ensuring that the causes and consequences of inequality go largely unquestioned. Without legitimation and justification, inequality, especially extreme inequality, is so offensive to a basic sense of fairness that it calls into question the moral order of society. The perpetuation of inequality requires an internalized view of the world where hierarchies based on ascription rather than merit are largely unquestioned.

The issue of enduring inequality is a matter of growing importance today. In the last 30 years the confluence of economy and politics has rewarded a small number of individuals and families at the top of society while most Americans have lost economic ground, some dramatically. A study by the Economic Policy Institute in 2012 found that between 1979 and 2007 the richest 10% of Americans garnered 91% of all new wealth. The top 1% has experienced what amounts to a turbo-charged rise in their wealth; the distribution of wealth in the United States today is more skewed in favor of the already wealthy than it has been at any other time in our history. The top 1% owns 38% of the nation's wealth; the top 96–99% owns over 21%; the top 90–95% owns over 11%; the bottom 40% owns 0.2%.

Upward mobility in the last 25 years has been so small as to be virtually immeasurable. In January 2012, *New York Times* reporter Jason DeParle examined the lack of mobility in American life and concluded, "at least five large studies in recent years have found the United States to be less mobile than comparable nations." The Economic Mobility Project at the Pew Charitable Trust found that 65% of those born in the bottom fifth of the income distribution stay in the bottom two-fifths (DeParle, 2012). Among industrialized nations, we are near the bottom in providing opportunities for those who did not win the birth lottery (Kalhenberg, 2000). It is the hope of many that this growing economic and social divide will be mitigated by education, but the evidence for this is weak from an enduring inequality perspective.

THE GREAT UNEQUALIZER

In February 2012, reporter Sabrina Tavernise wrote in the *New York Times*, "Now, in an analysis of long-term data published in recent months, researchers are finding that while the achievement gap between white and black students has narrowed significantly over the past decades, the gap between rich and poor students has grown substantially during the same period." Tavernise quotes Professor Sean Reardon of Stanford University: "We have moved from a society in the 1950s and 1960s, in which race was more consequential than family income, to one today in which family income appears more determinative of educational success than race." Reardon estimates that the achievement gap between students from the top 90th percentile of income and the bottom 10th percentile has grown 40% since the 1960s.

This state of affairs has not escaped scholars; there is an excellent tradition of research that looks at how inequality is reproduced *within* schools through tracking and other internal sorting and selection mechanisms (Alexander, Fennessey, McDill, & D'Amico, 1979; Delpit, 2006; Duncan, Featherman, & Duncan 1972; Heyns, 1974; Jencks & Brown, 1975; Lucas, 1999; McDill & Rigsby, 1973; Oakes, 2005). I recognize the importance of this form of educational stratification; but it is my belief that at the societal level differences *between* schools based on the class composition of their student bodies reproduces inequality in much the way a coin machine sorts different size coins—with unerring consistency (Coleman, Hoffer, & Kilgore, 1981; Finn, 2009; Kozol, 1991; Lewis & Wanner, 1979; Levine, 1980).

Contrary to popular belief, years of education as a measure of achievement do not always translate into upward class mobility because educational *amount* and educational *route* are two very different ways of thinking about educational mobility (Cookson & Persell, 1985; Turner, 1960). Educational amount is essentially a measure of academic seat time in an educational system where the barriers to academic promotion are very low and in some cases essentially nonexistent. Educational route is about with *whom* a student goes to school, the nature of his or her *socialization* experiences, and the *social power* of the credential with which he or she graduates in the transition to higher education and career. The fact that the last five candidates for president of the United States all graduated from private elite boarding schools should tell us something about the importance of educational routes.

THE PERSISTENCE OF CLASS

It is sometimes suggested that we are becoming a talent-based society rather than a class-based society (Friedman, 2007). If new businesses are invented in Palo Alto garages by high school students, have we not transcended class and arrived at a society where talent trumps family background as the agent of mobility? Isn't class an antiquated concept best tossed into the trash bin of history? The best answer to these questions is no, with the understanding that class structures evolve over time even if their basic structure remains intact. Just as the human body evolves over time, the class structure evolves, but slowly. (See Emile Durkheim [1956] for a very early sociological discussion of why social structure is not going away soon. For more recent work, see Aronowitz, 2003; Giddens, 1973; Olson, 1965; Parkin, 1974; Robinson, 1984; Rossides, 1976; Wrong, 1979.)

Howard Bloom in *Global Brain* (2000) cites convincing anthropological evidence that social hierarchies have existed for 25 million years. Mammals, in particular, are socially organized along social power grids; primates, including *Homo sapiens*, have very complex social systems based on competition, power, and status. Just as human DNA is encoded in a double helix inherited from past generations, our social DNA is encoded in an inherited social double helix of hierarchy and power. There are some well-respected sociologists such as Paul Kingston (2001) who argue that we live in a classless society, but I am convinced that class divisions will remain deep in the future.

Scholars debate about how to define and describe the American class structure, but one practical and empirically sound definition has been offered by Dennis Gilbert (2011): "Social classes are groups of families, more or less equal in rank and differentiated from other families above or below them with regard to characteristics such as occupation, income, wealth and prestige" (p. 11).

The American class system crystallized in the late 19th century (Aldrich, 1988). Prior to this period, the United States was a relatively impoverished rural society of small farmers with a small urban middle class and a small landed aristocracy. The Civil War changed that. Not only was slavery abolished but Northern industrialization spread quickly west on the railroads built during the war. Great fortunes were made by those who owned the railroads and later the emerging oil industry. This was the period when the current American class system took shape and the newly wealthy began to adopt the cultural artifacts and traditions of the British upper class. Much of this "new" money became today's old "money" as the class structure crystalized and solidified.

It is not the case, however, that the creation of a more or less permanent upper class has gone uncontested in American public life. As the wealth of the "Robber Baron" increased in the late 19th and early 20th centuries, resistance to their dominance arose. The Progressive Movement, most notably led by Theodore Roosevelt and Woodrow Wilson, challenged the unfettered economic and political power of the wealthy by passing laws such as the income tax in order to regulate wealth and to some degree limit the intergenerational transmission of wealth. When Franklin Roosevelt was elected president in 1932, he enacted several New Deal laws that regulated financial markets while at the same time began to establish a social safety net for all Americans. Social Security was the crowning achievement of the era.

The economic surge that the United States experienced after World War II led to a widely distributed rise in income; the period from roughly 1945 to 1975 was a period of shared prosperity when the class structure flattened considerably. Beginning in the mid-1970s, however, many New Deal financial regulations were rolled back and wealth began migrating upward at an accelerated rate until, today, we have the greatest concentration of wealth at the top of the class system than at any other time in American history. There has been a resurgence of class divisions fueled by the "new" money generated by the communications and service revolutions.

As a consequence, the current American class structure remains basically similar to the class structure developed in the age of early industrialization. Although there have been shifts within class divisions, the hierarchical organization of classes has remained stable. At the top of the pyramid is the upper class, consisting of less than 1% of Americans. This class is noted for its wealth, social prestige, traditions, and the capacity to pass on its status to its children and grandchildren regardless of the offsprings' abilities, ambitions, or inclinations. Recently, the wealthiest members of the upper class and their professional advisors have found their wealth doubling, even tripling, thanks to changes in the tax code, careful investment, and access to influential members of the federal government. It is not uncommon for members of this class to have annual incomes in excess of $2 million. In general, members of the upper class are able to live from their investments, but their dividends are often supplemented by membership on philanthropic and business boards, high-profile leadership positions, and partnerships in Wall Street brokerage houses.

The professional and business class, often referred to as the upper middle class, is composed of roughly 14% of Americans, and is the class of destination for those who are doctors, successful attorneys, high-level executives, and entrepreneurs. Upper-middle-class families earn over six figures annually, often into the millions. Many invest in the stock market, housing, and tangible capital goods such as cars, boats, second homes, art, jewelry, and fine wine. Members of the upper middle class are the managers of society in the profit and nonprofit sectors and have seen their class interests gain strength in the last 30 years due to changes in the economy, the social and financial value placed on elite educational credentials, and their close relationship with the upper class, particularly in gaining control of the national political system.

Below the upper middle class is the middle class. Most Americans think of themselves and their friends as middle class—to be in the middle of the social pyramid seems to be the cultural and political sweet spot in the American social imagination. Our political class makes defense of the middle class a reliable default position when all else fails. Middle-class people are considered typical Americans, although this cultural trope is largely a myth; from a class power perspective, the middle class is far from the dominant class. Comprising roughly 30% of the population, the middle class is composed of teachers, salespeople, social service workers, small business owners, mid-level government workers, and just about anyone who has a middle-income white-collar job. Their average annual income is $70,000; their home is their greatest and often only asset.

The working class consists roughly of 30% of Americans. Members of the working class are blue-collar union members, utility workers, farm laborers, tradesmen and tradeswomen, security workers, members of the enlisted military, firefighters, police officers, secretaries, and office clerks. Differences in income between the lower middle class and the upper working class are often negligible. Salaried and hourly members of the working class have little or no net worth; their average annual income is roughly $40,000. In many ways, the working class is America's invisible class; lacking prestigious educational credentials and sometimes holding what the upper and middle classes consider political incorrect social beliefs, members of the working class are often portrayed by the mainstream media as unenlightened and behind the times.

At the bottom of the working class the social safety net gets very tattered. For the 13% of Americans who are the working poor, life is very hard. They have virtually no assets, they are likely to earn roughly $25,000 annually, and the jobs they do have are unstable. They are the last to be hired and the first to be fired. Employed as low-level manual, retail, and service workers, they are likely to go through extended periods of unemployment. They often struggle to pay rent, and homelessness is an ever-present danger. They seldom have health insurance and are reliant on a system of public institutions that is increasingly underfunded or have disappeared in the last 2 decades.

The underclass or the poor consists of those individuals and families that have no secure position in the economy. The underclass earns on average less than $15,000 a year in part-time jobs. They must often rely on public assistance for survival. They do not own much of anything and in recent years have had few prospects for upward mobility. Overrepresented by people of color, single mothers, and immigrants, members of the underclass live in substandard housing, pick up day jobs when they can, often suffer from preventable diseases such as childhood asthma, and must move often in an effort to find work, housing, and safety. The life expectancy of the underclass is measurably shorter than that of other classes (Kawachi, Kennedy, Lochner, & Prothrow-Stith, 1997). Roughly 12% of Americans are underclass.

THE SOCIAL ORGANIZATION OF HIGH SCHOOLS

This brief overview of the major contours of today's class system provides us with a useful tool for understanding the social organization of high schools. Establishing the relationship between the organization of social classes and the social organization of high schools is central to this book's thesis. There are roughly 26,500 public and 10,700 private high schools in the United States, serving approximately 16 million students. At first glance, an observer might imagine that there is a wide array of high school options for American students. The United States is a large, multicultural nation with significant regional and local differences.

Intuitively, we might expect that attending high school in East Los Angeles or in rural Wisconsin would be very different experiences. Or that attending a high school run by a fundamentalist church would be dramatically different from attending a progressive arts school. Some high schools are large; some are small. Some high schools are cheerful; some are depressing. This picture is complicated further by the presence of a large Roman Catholic high school system, home schooling, charter schools, virtual schools, high schools run by juvenile justice systems, schools for dropouts, military schools, outward bound schools, and schools for the talented and gifted.

How could anyone create a typology out of this dizzying array?

The answer to this question is twofold. American high schools differ from each other in their secondary organizational and geographic characteristics, but are remarkably similar in their primary characteristics and class reproduction functions (Parsons, 1968; Powell, Farrar, & Cohen, 1985). No one would mistake a prep school for a working-class high school, and no one would mistake a high school in an upper-middle-class suburban neighborhood for a high school located in a poverty-stricken neighborhood of a big city.

But in important ways the vast majority of high schools do share certain characteristics; the core academic curricula of nearly all American high schools is similar because of state graduation requirements and college entrance policies. Almost all high schools draw their students from a pool of families that share very similar class characteristics. Generally, families want their class cultures to be incorporated into the classrooms and cultures in the schools their children attend.

As a result, our system of high schools is organized into a real-life class-based typology of schools. High schools array themselves along class divisions naturally because society is arrayed by class in what seems to many to be the natural order of things. To study how this array of schools reproduces the class system requires that we not get lost in the small differences between schools serving similar class, ethnic, and race constituencies, but instead focus on their essential ethos, academic philosophies, connections to the world of colleges, and even more important, their class cultures.

SNAPSHOT OF THE STUDY

When I undertook this research I realized that conventional data were not going to yield meaningful answers. To dig under the skin of the "presenting" school cultures and the rationalizations that accompany deep inequality, I decided to conduct a grassroots ethnographic study of institutions. I needed to see, hear, and understand the implicit, sometimes hidden, cultures of the schools. I am most interested in deep socialization; understanding how deep socialization takes place cannot be understood with a survey or by absorbing oneself in record data.

The proof points for this study are not dependent on anecdotal conversations, large-scale surveys, or quantitative analysis. My proof points come from a structured institutional and comparative analysis of five representative high schools:

- Highridge Academy, an elite private boarding school
- Meadowbrook High, located in a wealthy suburb
- Riverside High, located in a middle-class neighborhood
- Patrick Henry High, located in a working-class rural community
- Roosevelt High, located in one of the poorest urban congressional districts in the United States.

The names of the schools have been changed and I have not used the names of individual teachers, students, or administrators to ensure confidentiality. Moreover, it should be emphasized that these schools are representative of a set of similar schools. This is not an exposé of individual schools; it is a study of how American high schools create enduring inequality through their socialization processes.

My basic methodology is a type of school portraiture, an approach first developed by Sara Lawrence-Lightfoot (1983). This approach for understanding the inner life of schools is powerful because it helps us draw a picture of a school, revealing its institutional practices and culture as they actually occur. By using direct comparative techniques, the class-related features of a school's organization and ethos can be distinguished, compared, and clarified. My argument is based on data and logic in equal amounts because without a strong theoretical framework to guide questioning and observation, it is difficult to weave a story that touches on those aspects of schooling that are hidden and often denied.

My hope is that this work will introduce readers to the real roadblocks to basic educational and social justice and that readers will be motivated to call into question the assumptions of the powerful about the legitimacy of our current organization of schooling. When we can honestly confront the real obstacles facing us, perhaps we can begin the process of bending education in the direction of justice. One anonymous reviewer of this book's original manuscript wondered if my hope that we can build an equitable educational system squared with the book's thesis and data. Do middle-, upper-middle-, and upper-class Americans really want a fair and meritocratic school system? Is it not in their interest to "game" the system to their advantage?

Perhaps so. But we will make little progress as a society if we don't aspire to a transcendent ideal that is inclusive and innovative (Cookson, 2011). Despite the current facts on the ground, I am an optimist. The United States has gone through many cycles of social regression and progression. It is my hope that we are entering a period of progress and greater equality. It is worth mentioning that in 1932 George Counts of Teachers College delivered three lectures to the Progressive Education Association, later published as *Dare the School Build a New Social Order?* It is time to ask this question again.

CHAPTER OVERVIEW

Class Rules consists of seven chapters: Chapter 1, *Collective Memory and Class Reproduction*, lays out the book's central argument and research strategy. Chapters 2 through 6 describe in detail the five different class-based high school rites of passage. Chapter 7, *Bending History Toward Justice*, summarizes the findings, examines their implications, and outlines an alternative policy framework to mainstream educational reform. A methodological appendix and references are included.

1

Collective Memory and Class Reproduction

Memory is the core of what we call reality.
—Howard Bloom

INTRODUCTION: AMANDA, SALLY, AND VIVIAN

Meet three young women about to graduate from high school—Amanda, Sally, and Vivian. Amanda is graduating from a socially elite New England prep school, Sally is graduating from a working-class high school in Cleveland, and Vivian is graduating from a high school located in the poorest neighborhood in the Bronx. All three have studied the same core subjects, all have grade point averages in the top quartile of their class, all have completed state graduation requirements, all are diligent students, all have scored above average on standardized tests, and all want to be successful. Each of them is brimming with hope and expectation. Each of them is earnest and energetic. As they walk down the aisle to receive their high school diplomas, they are smiling and pleased. They look forward to the future with great expectations.

But then reality rushes in.

Amanda has the full force of her prep school behind her. She has been groomed for success. Her college application has been carefully edited and over the summer her parents hired a tutor to give her inside tips about taking the SAT exam. But Amanda has even a better edge than her summer tutor when it comes to competing for a place in a highly selective college or university. She has her school. Her school is powerful and is noted for serving the country's most elite families (Cookson, 1981; Hopper, 1971; Kamens, 1977). She is certified to have the right social stuff (DiMaggio, 1982). Moreover, her school has deep connections to the admissions offices at the most selective and socially desirable colleges (Cookson, 1981; Cookson & Persell, 1985). The school's college counselors and the college admissions officers are a phone call or email away. Amanda has the huge social asset of her institution behind her. There is better than a 95% chance that Amanda will graduate from college.

Sally is the first in her family to apply to college. She did not receive any extra help taking standardized exams and she filled out her college applications herself. The lone college guidance counselor at her high school graduated from a local state college and simply hands Sally some college brochures whenever they meet. Sally is on her own. Her school has no social power and is off the radar screen for the admissions officers at selective colleges. If Sally does attend college, there is a less than a 50% chance that she will graduate (Roy, 2005).

Vivian has an even steeper educational hill to climb. There is no real college guidance department at her school, and only the local community college sends recruiters each spring. Some in her family want her to start working right away; without a sizable scholarship Vivian can't afford college anyway. Her school has no social power; in fact, most college admissions officers are only dimly aware of her school's existence and what they have heard is not good. Far from helping Vivian to realize her dream, her school is an obstacle—one she will most likely not overcome. If she does attend college, there is less than a 30% chance that she will graduate (Roy, 2005).

And Vivian is in the top quartile of her class; if she were in the middle two quartiles, she would have only an 8% chance of graduating; if she were in the lowest quartile, she would have a 3% chance of graduating. Sally's odds are only slightly better: If she were in the middle two quartiles, she would have a 21% chance of graduating and if she were in the lowest quartile, she would have only a 7% chance (Roy, 2005).

On the other hand, if Amanda were to graduate from a public school, she would still have a 74% chance of graduating from college because of her class background. If she were an average student, she would have a 51% chance of graduating and even if she were a poor student, she still would have a 30% chance of graduating (Roy, 2005).

In other words, where you go to high school matters. And it matters a lot. When the birth lottery and educational stratification meet, the result is a social class sorting and selection machine that consistently reproduces class differences. Amanda, Sally, and Vivian are destined to live in worlds apart. Advantage is a cumulative process, as is disadvantage; the process of rewarding and punishing children based on their parents' wealth and social status begins at birth. Secondary schools and colleges accelerate advantage and disadvantage by channeling, legitimating, and credentializing as objective successes the cultural achievements of the advantaged and discarding and delegitimizing the cultural achievements of the disadvantaged. This process is not the result of evil people, or an invisible hand, or some worldwide conspiracy. It is the result of structure and people going about the unconscious business of class reproduction.

PART ONE: UNPACKING CLASS RITES OF PASSAGE

As I indicated in the Introduction, my task is to understand how high schools perpetuate and reinforce the American class system. I see the process of class reproduction as a series of interrelated elements mentioned in the Introduction and elaborated below.

How It Works, Part One: Chartering and Status Rights

High schools are social and emotional hothouses. They are intense human environments where relationships are created, broken, reunited, and recycled. In the 1990s, a group of researchers at the Claremont University released a report based on an in-depth study of four Southern California schools. They spent 18 months in the schools collecting thousands of pages of transcripts, essays, drawings, journal entries, and notes from 4,000 students, 1,000 parents, and 200 teachers, administrators, and other school staff.

The researchers expected to file a report about teaching and many of the issues related to fulfilling the public mission of the schools. What they found instead was that the most commonly cited problem by the people in the schools was the nature of their relationship with each other. How other people affected the respondent was far more important than what the school bulletin said or what the chair of the school board pronounced about the lofty goals of education. Although the researchers did not intend to, they validated the observation of the founder of American sociology of education Willard Waller (1932), "The most important things that happen in schools result in the interaction of personalities . . . schools are despotisms in a state of perilous equilibrium" (p. 11). The poet e. e. cummings said the same thing simply, "feeling is first."

Schools, particularly high schools, are the emotional soup from which we draw many of our life lessons, some of which never leave us. We remember the biology teacher who taught us about Darwin by dressing up like the sage himself; we remember the track coach who told us we could run faster if only we tried harder; we remember the teenage romantic crushes and being rejected; and we remember graduation day. But behind all the specific memories is the memory of belonging to a powerful high school culture. This all-embracing culture forged inside of us a sense of who we are with a set of defined possibilities and limitations. We developed a collective identity out of the actual encounters we experienced. High school is a 6,000-hour experience; is it surprising that schools should stamp the consciousness of their students?

Society recognizes that graduates from different schools have different class identities. Sociologist John Meyer (1977) offered a cogent explanation of why we recognize these school status differences: "In modern society success is assigned to persons on the basis of duration and type of education, holding constant what they have learned in school" (p. 59). He maintains that schools, as part of an institutional system, influence individuals' lives above and beyond their ability to teach students academic skills. Schools vary by their institutional authority.

From this observation, Meyer developed the concept of the school "charter," which he primarily applied to colleges but can be usefully applied to high schools (Cookson, 1981). Meyer (1972) defines charter as follows:

> An institutional agreement that a given program, college or system of colleges is to produce and does produce a certain kind of person. It is institutionalized in the sense that knowledgeable and authoritative people generally take it for granted and act on it. (p. 111)

Students, according to Meyer (1977), "Tend to adopt personal and social qualities appropriate to the positions to which their schools are charted to assign them" (p. 60). For example, graduates from West Point are chartered to be army officers; seminaries are chartered to produce religious clerics; art schools produce artists. These graduates have "status rights." These status rights are a form of cultural capital that has market and social value. Sociologist David Kamens explains (1977):

> Schools symbolically redefine people and make them eligible for membership in societal categories to which specific sets of rights are assigned, e.g., income. The social organization of schools is a major symbolic index of the kind of socialization that has occurred and thus legitimates the conferral of specific status rights. (pp. 217–218)

Applying this perspective to high school graduates across the social class spectrum is helpful in understanding why *where* a student goes to school can shape his or her life chances. Graduating from an elite private school confers different status rights from graduating from a school in a community of concentrated poverty or even from a school in an upper-middle-class suburb (see Hollingshead's 1949 early ethnography about the impact of social class on youth). These status rights are not just symbolic; they influence life chances. Colleges and universities evaluate high schools not only by their curricula and academic cultures but also by a number of other factors, including the social status of the school measured by the status of the school's parent body (Cookson, 1981).

The chartering effect reaches beyond the high school to college transition; it echoes throughout individuals' lives. In Meyer's words again (quoted in Sadovnik, 2001):

It is argued that people in modern societies are allocated to adult roles on the basis of years and types of education, apart from anything they have learned in schools. Education, in allocation theory, is a set of institutional rules which legitimately classify and authoritatively allocate individuals to positions in society. The power of the allocation idea arises from its obvious empirical validity. We all know that status positions in modern societies are assigned on the basis of education. (p. 135)

I would add only this to Meyer's insights: Allocation without socialization would lead to a very unstable social system. Human beings do not think of themselves as being allocated by institutional rules (even if they are); they fervently want to believe that their lives have meaning and that they have free will. Without a theory of the intrapsychic processes of acceptance, rejection, and reconciliation, allocation theory cannot explain change, resistance, and the silent suffering of those who are allocated to positions of powerlessness. Allocation is not the result of every newborn being labeled; it is the result of power relations. We are careful observers; we know our social positions and fear being ostracized and exiled. These intrapsychic processes might seem nearly impossible to identify because they can appear gossamer and speculative. But in actuality this is not the case; they are as apparent as the nose on our collective face.

Those of us who haven't been in a school for many years or have repressed our memories of the social/emotional hothouses that high schools are might be wondering if high schools really have the kind of socialization power I am ascribing to them. After all, many adolescents in American society appear to be *undersocialized* rather than systematically socialized (Coleman, 1961). Is that kid with his baseball cap askew really undergoing a class rite of passage? Are those students hanging out in the parking lot really being infused with class consciousness? Aren't adolescents more likely to resist authority than submit to it? And what about social networking? Do high school students really identify with other kids of their class background in an age of democratic communication? To fully answer these questions, we need to understand the socializing power of schools.

In 1979, Michael Rutter and his colleagues published *Fifteen Thousand Hours: Secondary Schools and Their Effects on Children*. In many ways, this was a groundbreaking work because the authors asked some fundamental questions about schooling that anticipated this study: "Does a child's experiences at school have any effect; does it matter *which* school he [*sic*] goes to; and what are the features of a school that matter?" (p. 1). Rutter and his co-authors' conclusion that schools do matter should not come as a shock; in fact, Rutter and his associates found that schools play a very significant role in either promoting or hindering student achievement. At the time this study was published it created quite a stir because it was a large-scale study that called into question the findings of James Coleman and his associates (1966) that school effects were small when compared with family effects. The finding of the Rutter et al. study, however, that is most relevant to this study is his conclusion:

> People tend to act on the basis of their psychological identification with particular groups rather than keeping with any formal membership of organizations or attendance at institutions. For this purpose, the social group is the real or imaginary collective, whose perspective is assumed by the individual. (p. 194)

Rutter and his colleagues were not looking at class differences; they were interested in "academic acceptance." What they discovered, however, provides evidence that schools create collective consciousnesses in the form of school memories.

How It Works, Part Two: The Formation of Class Consciousness

Even though the term *class consciousness* sounds esoteric and academic, the concept is straightforward. We know that class differences exist. The question is—do members of a class have a sense of their own class position? Karl Marx (Gilbert, 2011) distinguished between a *class-in-itself* and a *class-for-itself*. A class-in-itself is merely a collection of individuals who may share a similar objective situation but have no sense of a shared destiny.

A class-for-itself is conscious of a shared set of interests and a shared destiny. When objective class position leads to a shared class consciousness, the possibility of collective action in defense of those interests and values is heightened. A class-for-itself is an intergenerational collectivity that shares a meaning system. Class loyalty is like a religious conviction—it defines who we are in a way that is not always easily understood through reason alone (Wexler, Crichlow, Kern, & Matusewicz, 1992).

The power of group and class loyalty is not merely a theoretical construct; it has been demonstrated empirically. In a 2009 article, *Commonality and the Complexity of "We": Social Attitudes and Social Change*, social psychologists John Dovidio, Samuel Gaertner, and Tamar Saguy studied the fundamental and complex role of collective identity in the formation of intergroup biases and disparities. They developed what they call the "common ingroup identity model" based on social identity theory. This line of research makes clear that people derive personal esteem from their membership in groups and strive to establish the positive distinctiveness of their group relative to other groups. The authors conclude (2009):

The psychological power of creating common identity, a sense of "we," is impressive. Categorizing others as members of one's group has a profound impact. Spontaneously, people think more deeply about and feel closer to and more positive about members of their own group (the ingroup) than members of other groups (the outgroups). People dismiss the negative actions of ingroup members, communicate in ways that maintain positive orientations toward them, and create a psychological platform for bias against outgroup members. In addition, people are more open with, trusting of, and helpful to ingroup members than to outgroup members. (p. 14)

Class membership creates a sense of social identity in industrial societies that is foundational and basic. This does not mean that everyone in the same class thinks alike about everything. Members of the upper class, for example, may have different views on social issues such as abortion or gay marriage. But they are very likely to agree about defending a tax code that protects their wealth. Members of the upper middle class may disagree about American foreign policy, but they are very likely to agree that educational credentials ought to be the basis of professional certification. In a similar vein, working-class families have a collective interest in the maintenance of a living wage. Working-class individuals and groups may differ about the place of religion in schools, but they are likely to share similar ideas about the value of physical labor and the importance of a fair tax code. Families who are dependent on public assistance for survival may vary in terms of their cultural tastes, but they are likely to share the same perspective in the defense of the government's role in maintaining social safety nets.

It is often suggested by social theorists that the upper class is a class-for-itself, but the other classes have, at best, only the weakest sense of being classes-for-themselves. This proposition is worth examining. I suspect that we lack sufficient data across classes to assess adequately the underlying class consciousness of nonelites. I also suspect that class consciousness is expressed differently in different classes. An upper-class man or woman may express class consciousness in one manner (such as buying an expensive painting to hang above his or her couch) while a middle-class man or woman may express his or her class consciousness in another manner (for example, by buying a Van Gogh poster to hang in the kitchen); but that does not mean that the middle-class individual is less conscious of his or her class than the upper-class individual.

Hopefully, this research will shed some light on this issue. My experience tells me that all families and individuals are aware of class and its consequence in their lives. But relative powerlessness and absolute powerlessness make collective class action difficult and dangerous. An upper-class businessman or -woman can pick up a phone (or have someone pick it up for them) to get what he or she wants; a poor person has to take to the streets in protest and in doing so runs into the power of the state in the form of the police who are publicly sworn to defend private property and informally dedicated to protecting the ownership classes.

Measuring class consciousness presents a host of methodological issues. As far as I know, we don't have any reliable measures of consciousness in general and none that measure class consciousness, at least in a quantifiable sense. Some researchers, however, have attempted to study how class affects childrearing practices (Halwachs, 1959; Hollingshead, 1949; Kohn, 1969, 1976; Kohn & Schooler, 1983; Lareau, 2003). In the late 1960s, Melvin Kohn and his associates asked parents from an international sample to select from a list of characteristics those they considered most desirable in a child of the same sex and age as their own child. Although all parents chose some desirable characteristics such as being happy, there were notable social class differences in other responses.

Middle-class parents were more likely to choose "curiosity" over "obedience" than working-class parents. Kohn found a pattern of responses that seemed to indicate that middle-class parents favored imagination and creativity in their developing children, while working-class parents favored obedience and conformity. He interpreted this to mean that middle-class parents are interested in the internal dynamics of growth in their children, whereas working-class parents are more interested in external control.

Kohn's work, as groundbreaking as it was, was drawn from a narrow slice of the class structure, and I suspect that in terms of identifying the distinctive and important features of class consciousness his approach partially confuses cultural conformity with an internalized sense of class position and class structure. Working-class adolescents are not noted for their rigid conformity despite some of their parents' wishes, and not all middle-class students are noted for their creativity and individualism.

Annette Lareau (2003) also used interview data to compare the childrearing practices of middle-class and working-class parents; she and her team put in thousands of hours observing what the parents actually did with her children. She found that middle- and upper-middle-class parents managed their children's development carefully—a process she labeled "cultivated growth." Working-class parents, on the other hand, were far less structured in their approach to childrearing. She labeled their approach "natural growth."

From these observations, Lareau drew conclusions about the class-based nature of childrearing in the areas of the organization of daily activities, language development, and relations with schools. She believes that the cultivated growth strategy used by middle- and upper-middle-class families encourages a sense of entitlement in their children. Entitlement is a useful concept when constructing a working theory of class consciousness because when one feels entitled, one is less likely to feel guilty about unearned privileges and is more likely to see society through some very selective social bifocals.

Feeling entitled, however, is not the same as class consciousness. Men may feel entitled in gender relations and White people may feel entitled in relation to people of color, but these forms of unearned entitlement do not equate to class consciousness. We know that prejudice is a learned characteristic, but is class consciousness learned at an early age? This is largely an unexplored area of study, but there has been some interesting research. For instance, in 1949 Celia Stendler embarked on a fascinating study of the social perceptions of 6th-graders in a small town in New England. She presented them pictures of class items such as an English riding habit, a well-furnished room, torn clothing, and different occupational activities. When asked to place their friends in one of three classes based on the pictures, the children agreed 70% of the time with adults who also rated the same items according to class.

Gilbert (2011) has drawn together a number of studies that strongly suggest that by the time a child reaches the age of 12 he or she mirrors the class perspectives of the adults around him or her and has a very accurate sense of the class structure. For instance, Simmons and Rosenberg (1971) showed that 3rd-graders from Baltimore City Schools were able to rank 15 occupations in nearly the same order as adults. Tutor (1991) showed 1st-, 4th-, and 6th-graders photographs of upper-, middle- , and lower-class people. She asked them to group them according to families and match them with cars and houses. Even the 1st-graders were able to successfully make the appropriate matches; by the 6th grade the matches the children made were nearly perfect.

Leahy (1981, 1983a, 1983b) found that children between 7 and 17 develop increasingly sophisticated conceptions of class. Young children think of being rich and poor in physical terms; as children grow into young adulthood they think more in psychological terms. Joe, age 6, said, "Poor people have no food. They won't have no Thanksgiving. They don't have nothing. . . . Rich people have crazy outfits and poor people have no outfits." Dean, age 12, was a bit more complex in his assessment of class relations: "I think that rich and poor people should all be the same, each have the same amount of money because then the rich people won't think they are so big" (Gilbert, 2011, pp. 101–102).

Although these studies are hardly definitive, they are instructive. From research and experience, we can feel fairly sure that children and adolescents are aware of class differences. It is a sad truth that we learn at a very early age about inequality and, in Joe's words, we learn that poor people "won't have no Thanksgiving." But how does this awareness become internalized in a way that shapes an adolescent's social worldview?

Research on adolescent socialization and social class. The question of how adolescents interpret class and their position in the hierarchy of classes has interested sociologists for over 50 years (Cookson, 2009a, 2009b, 2010; Flanagan & Campbell, 2003; Havinghurst & Taba, 1949; Hummelweit, Halsey, & Oppenheim, 1952; Rosenberg & Pearlin, 1978). In 1949, Richard Centers published *The Psychology of Social Classes: A Study of Class Consciousness* in which he found that objective social class position and subjective social class identification were correlated among adults. Centers found in his study of adolescents that subjective social class identification is present among teenagers and they tend to identify upward. Significantly, he found that as people mature their understanding about their class position becomes more realistic.

In the early 1970s, sociologist Alan Kerckhoff published *Socialization and Social Class.* He began his study with a clear position (1972), "The process by which an individual finds his adult place [*sic*] in society occurs within the context of the pre-existent social structure" (p. v). In writing of the social class socialization of adolescents, he emphasized the importance of high schools (1972), "The social context within the individual spends his adolescence is as important as the personal qualities he has developed earlier. What kind of high school he goes to, for instance, makes a great deal of difference" (p. 99). Addressing the question of the intergenerational transmission of class position, Kerchkoff (1972) continues, "We have thus seen how the socialization process varies by social class, and this variation would lead us to expect a great deal of continuity in social class placement from one generation to the next" (p. 121). He convincingly shows that students' attitudes toward education vary by class and that adults treat students differently according to class.

As important as this early work is, it suffers somewhat from an underdeveloped sense of the stratification of high schools and ignores the importance of the top of the class structure. Without an institutional analysis of the full range of high schools by the class composition of their student bodies, we run the risk of getting a truncated view of the transmission of class privilege and the processes of reproducing enduring inequality.

This weakness is also found in more recent research. In 2000, Elizabeth Goodman and her colleagues published *Adolescents' Understanding of Social Class: A Comparison of White Upper Middle Class and Working Class Youth.* In this study the authors reported that working-class youth and upper-middle-class youth varied in terms of perceptions, aspirations for the future, and expectations for achieving their aspirations. The report implied that working-class youth are not as far-thinking as their upper-middle-class peers but, once again, the range of classes studied is limited.

A scholar who has developed a sophisticated approach to uncovering how adolescents construct their social worlds is Ellen Brantlinger (1993a, 1993b). She found in her ethnographic study of high school students that social conflict is ubiquitous in schools; schools are not neutral settings; social perceptions are shaped through what she calls *school discourse*. She found that low-income students are systematically humiliated and ostracized by other students. In fact, school for low-income students is just short of a living hell.

None of these studies, however, addresses the challenge of trying to uncover how class consciousness is forged. To meaningfully approach that problem, we need to turn our research gaze from the individual to the network of institutions that process and allocate students by their social class. Schools are the institutional matrixes by which the awareness of class differences is forged into class consciousness. But how does this happen? In what ways do schools contribute to a sense of class solidarity? What is the social class bridge between family and school? What actually happens in schools to transform generalized class perceptions into specific class positions?

To answer these questions, we need to unpack the complex and sometimes hidden relationship between class reproduction and education. I suggest that the internalization of class relations by students forms the structure of their intellectual and emotional framework for understanding the world around them. This process consists of intense class-based rites of passage that *infuse* adolescents with the values, dispositions, and beliefs of their class.

You will not find these rites of passage in schools' mission statements. You will not hear principals talking about class infusion. Class reproduction is not listed as one of the Common Core State Standards. In fact, almost nobody discusses this function of schooling, but it is very real.

How It Works, Part Three:
Collective Memory and School Rites of Passage

To understand how deep socialization occurs in school settings, we need a new perspective on adolescent development that will enable us to untangle the web of interactions that constitute the culture of schools. Schools are sites of learning, sites of social reproduction, and sites for conscious and unconscious communication. The culture of the school is the culture of transference, countertransference, denial, and possibility. Schools are rich in human experience, which is why their cultures are so delicate, mysterious, and complex.

The drama of schooling. One way to express this insight is to think of schools as fictional narratives in which all the participants play their parts and in doing so internalize the feelings, thoughts, and behaviors of their assigned roles, much the same way a method actor becomes a character in a play or movie. Few sociologists look to the famed 19th-century Russian actor and director Konstantin Stanislavsky for insights into class reproduction, but Stanislavsky understood how good actors use their emotional memory to develop their characters *from within*. By utilizing real memories, actors enter into a scene not from the beginning of a story but, as in life, as part of a continuum of experience. We learn the culture of school by playing a part that has been largely assigned to us.

In 1968, sociologist Robert Dreeben wrote a landmark essay entitled "The Contribution of Schooling to the Learning of Norms." He argued:

> It is my contention that the traditional conception of schooling as an instructional process, primarily cognitive in nature, is at best only partially tenable. That is, what pupils learn is in part some function of what is taught; but what *is* learned and from what experiences remain open questions. (p. 212)

In our research, Caroline Persell and I (1985) discovered that there was a striking difference between what is taught and what is learned in elite private schools. The official culture and student culture of a school teaches very different lessons about the meaning and exercise of power. The conflict inherent in school cultures causes students to internalize the story of their schooling in ways that often last a lifetime. Think of the emotions around class reunions and the reliving of youthful high jinks by aging alums. It is more than sentimentality; it is the rerun of a movie that was filmed years ago and etched into the hearts of graduates.

These are our collective memories. Memory is the process of recalling to mind facts previously learned. But it can also be the totality of one's experience. This totality is emotional and causes us to feel as though past events are not just in the past but still alive within us. These memories can be joyful when we remember the birth of a child or they can be painful when we remember the death of a loved one. Generally, our memories are shared experiences. Our memories are populated by other people. We swap stories, we laugh together, we cry together. Memories tell the stories of our collective lives. Memories define who we are. Nearly all of us have strong memories of school. When we share memories of institutional experiences, they become metaphorical and frame past and present experience (Morgan, 1986). The drama of schooling can be thought of as a kaleidoscope of emotions that are contagious.

School metaphors can vary from a machine, to a body, to a family, to a factory. These organizational metaphors provide a framework for understanding the interactions within the school. Because schools are the sum total of a network of intense relationships, I see schools as theaters of scripted interactions where students, teachers, and administrators create dramas and comedies according to scenes that are written into the cultural life and academic infrastructure of the school. Sociologist Mary Metz (2003) describes her school research as though she were witnessing a play called *Real School*. She describes the enormous social energy invested in the creation of this drama.

The fictional narratives of schools are emotionally charged. There is no mathematical precision for observing and understanding human feelings, interactions, and behaviors. The German social theorist Max Weber wrestled with the methodological problem of objectivity in social science. Because we cannot stand out of society and because we cannot honestly pretend that we are "value free," there is always the risk that we will project onto our research subjects our own fears, hopes, and confusions. Weber developed a concept he called *verstehen*, or understanding. We are capable of understanding meanings and values when they are causally linked. Theory allows us to connect the dots of human interaction in ways that are testable because human behavior is not random—it is structured by society. The micro (the individual) is emotionally mapped onto the macro (the society). The emotional transferences within schools are not random or casual; they are structured by an unspoken and invisible social framework that reflects the social framework of the larger society. We learn to be class actors through being exposed to our schools' deep curriculum of class formation.

Class rites of passage and ceremonies of control. The question that is sometimes left unanswered by even the most astute observers and theoreticians of education is just *how* the process of class reproduction takes place in our system of schools. I suggest that we learn our class position by undergoing certain class rites of passage that define who we are, give meaning to a confusing world, and stamp our thinking—they are the medium that drives collective memory into consciousness. Rites of passage are not one-dimensional or linear—they are dialectical and complex. They structure thought, feelings, and behavior. Deep socialization teaches us what we think is true about people and the ways of the world.

The drama of schooling is the story of children's and adolescents' rites of passage from family to society. These rites of passage are especially intense during adolescence. The idea that there is a special time of life called adolescence was invented by American social scientists and psychologists in the late 19th century. Before then, one was either a child or an adult, and even that line was not too firmly drawn. In *Rites of Passage: Adolescence in America 1790 to the Present* (1977), historian Joseph Kett describes how in the late 1890s adolescence was "discovered" by G. Stanley Hall and his colleagues at Clark University. Hall described adolescence as a second birth and a time of "storm and stress." In Hall's view, adolescence was a time of idealism, discovery, and openness to religious conversion. This belief that adolescence is a unique period of development is still with us today. Identifying, categorizing, and explaining why teenagers behave as they do is a small but thriving industry.

A rite of passage is meant to mold people in a particular image. When we see this taking place at a seminary or military school we grasp this concept immediately. Standing in the corridor of a local high school, this concept might be a little fuzzy. Most high school students seem a far cry from the seminarian or cadet. But looks can be deceptive; socialization does not require a uniform—socialization happens from the inside out. Every adolescent undergoes a rite of passage when his or her childhood identity is refashioned into a young adult identity. Ritual, symbolism, and metaphor are elements in the meaning systems we learn while undergoing a rite of passage. They are ceremonies of control designed to create a collective identity.

Although these rites of passage can take place in the home, on the playground, and in places of worship, in advanced industrial and postindustrial societies it is the school that is the primary and most powerful socializing agency. Children and adolescents literally spend thousands of hours in school, learning about the world from the school system, teachers, coaches, administrators, and other students. Just as nobody "teaches" the young to speak their native language, no one person "teaches" young people their sense of society—they learn it through the sum total of their experiences, fears, hopes, confusions, conscious strivings, and unconscious drives.

Class awareness and consciousness are reinforced by what we study and with whom. Not all school curricula are equal. The curricula for the children of the wealthy are enriched and demanding; the curricula for the children of the working class and poor are minimal and boring. The children of the wealthy learn to use complex and heavily class-coded language while other children learn a stripped-down style of communication, often based on popular media. Curricula contain explicit and implicit social codes: Am I a maker of history or simply an observer? Is the history of Western civilization my story or the story of White privilege? Is history made by men and not women? Do I learn the fundamental skills of higher-order thinking or do I fill out worksheets every day? Is my linguistic code complex and imaginative or am I schooled to be silent? Am I confident of my abilities or am I insecure and unsure of my worth? And, most important for this study, am I empowered or disempowered as an active social actor? Will I give orders or receive them? Will anyone ever care what I think, feel, or do?

How It Works, Part Four: The Process of Class Infusion

Recently, the subject of adolescent socialization has become a hot academic and research topic. Much of the newest research focuses on brain development and what neuroscientist Joseph LeDoux (2003) refers to as the "synaptic self." LeDoux (2003) argues that the interaction between nature and nurture creates synaptic changes in the brain: "Let's start with a fact: people don't come preassembled, but are glued together by life. And each time one of us is constructed, a different result occurs" (p. 3).

The argument that each of us is "wired" differently strikes me as questionable. When it comes to behavior, we are remarkably predictable and although we might style ourselves as the authors of our unique selves, the reality is that, generally, we are more alike than different when it comes to our values, dispositions, and actions. To cite Howard Bloom again (2000), behavior is contagious in the form of *behavioral memes* in which we observe each other and copy each other if the observed behavior results in more security or social and physical advantage. Behavioral memes can be thought of as norms. Normative behavior is not determined genetically; it is determined socially.

Sociology recognizes the role of nature in shaping the human experience (after all, we are mammals), but most sociologists believe that the self is socially constructed (Goffman, 1959; Miller, 1982). One of the early founders of sociology, George Herbert Mead (Miller, 1982), established this frame for understanding human behavior when he wrote, "the individual mind can exist only in relation to other minds with shared meaning" (p. 5). Mead believed that the self develops in relation to others; that is, human nature is socially constructed within the constraints of evolution. Mead explained, "Social consciousness is organized from the outside in. The social precepts which first arise are those of other selves" (Miller, 1982, p. 35). Mead's insights are useful to us because he offers us an important insight about how social control is internalized:

> Whenever we come to the question of social control, we find that it is recognized in this conscious attitude of others toward the self, in criticism or approval. We are constantly carrying about in us this self which is seen through the eyes of others, and this is being criticized. This constitutes the process of social control. (Miller, 1982, p. 72)

For Mead, the consciousness of the individual is a reflection of his or her social situation; our inner lives are socially constructed, as is our consciousness. Erving Goffman (1959, 1961) advanced Mead's interactional perspective by arguing for a dramaturgical perspective for understanding everyday life. Goffman's symbolic interactionalism emphasizes the role people assume in public life and how each of us tends to wear a public mask to influence others and perhaps to conceal our true intentions.

We know that the transition from childhood to young adulthood is a time of individuation, intellectual and physical growth, sexual awakening, and brain development. Psychologist Erik Erikson (1963) describes the period of time between 12 and 18 as the struggle between identity and role confusion. The struggle for identity, especially in a society that elevates personal success, is central to the adolescent's project of becoming an adult (Csikszentmihalyi & Larson, 1984). Most theories of development assume an individualistic model of identity. We live in a society where the master narrative reflects the goals and aspirations of striving individuals (Chubb & Moe, 1990; Frank & Cook, 1995; Friedman, 1962).

But theories of development that ignore power relations and the complex ways students internalize social relations only tell half the story. Adolescents are very sensitive to what others think and very often they establish their own identities through group identities such as clubs, sports, and gangs. Identity and assimilation are really two sides of the same developmental coin. Sociologist Sanford Dornbush (1955) defined assimilation as "a process of interpenetration and fusion in which persons and groups acquire the memories, sentiments, and attitudes of other persons and groups, and, by sharing their experience and history, are incorporated with them in a common cultural life" (p. 316).

Dornbush's concept of fusion takes us one step closer to understanding how the formation of class consciousness through class rites of passage may take place. Fusion means a melting together of two or more different elements, uniting them in a new form. I would argue, however, that in terms of meeting the social and emotional needs of adolescents, we need a stronger concept to explain how class relations are internalized. Deep socialization is more like psychic surgery than cosmetic alterations. We are, in Howard Bloom's phrase (2000), "social learning machines" (p. 42).

To understand how we incorporate society into our conscious and unconscious lives, we need an intrapsychic explanation that includes the whole person. The concepts of assimilation and merger may explain why military officers take on the caste features characteristic of military hierarchies, but in terms of acquiring class loyalty, these concepts only scratch the surface. We need a concept that is explanatory of the commitments and contradictions associated with class identity.

My perspective is that the internalization of class relations is similar to baptism, where identity is formed not by merger but by submersion. To clarify how baptism and submersion might give substance to an adolescent's class rite of passage, we might borrow profitably from a field of inquiry that specializes in baptism and submersion, so to speak. Infusion, in the theological sense, is the process whereby an individual is filled with the spirit of God. One who is infused with faith cannot meaningfully distinguish his or her inner life from that of God. The essence of infusion, from a socialization perspective, is that one merges with an identity larger than oneself, which in turn, requires a giving up of aspects of the self, perhaps in ways that may not even be conscious. One is infused with class consciousness, which becomes a seamless psychic garment, clothing the inner life of adolescents with a set of beliefs that are experienced as authentic and aligned with reality. Adolescents infused with class consciousness can hardly imagine an alternative social ecology.

Class infusion explains the chartering effect of high schools. We come to think of ourselves in ingrained ways that are generally congruent with what our schools intend us to be. Of course, there is resistance and occasionally rebellion, but the vast majority of us do not resist or rebel except in small symbolic ways that have little lasting impact. The truth is that most people gladly embrace their schools' charter.

How It Works, Part Five: Cultural Capital and the Deep Curriculum

Although the concept of infusion may be novel when applied to secular socialization, there is a long tradition of critical thinkers who have noted the role of schools in the transmission of social position. Socialist thinker Louis Althusser conceived of schools as the most important "ideological state apparatus" because of their role in ensuring the reproduction of class relations, and the Italian revolutionary Antonio Gramsci convincingly argued that cultural hegemony disguises the power of the dominate classes by excluding from educational discourse and consciousness alternative ways of knowing (to borrow a contemporary phrase). Gramsci's concept of cultural hegemony is very similar to the more contemporary concept of cultural capital.

The late French sociologist Pierre Bourdieu (1984) provocatively advanced the argument that there is an intimate and dynamic relationship between cultural capital and educational reproduction. According to Bourdieu and other critical thinkers, we adapt to the class cultures we belong to and in doing so acquire different forms and amounts of cultural capital. Cultural capital is made up of our symbolic assets, which we use to distinguish ourselves from others. At a very obvious level this determines what we eat, how we dress, what we read, the forms of culture we admire, and the values we place on educational credentials.

Cultural capital, however, is both a noun and a verb; one owns it and one exercises it. Education is the key variable in the development and exercise of cultural capital. Power is transmitted through a set of cultural relay stations that act as enormous distribution systems. Bourdieu's concept of how power is transmitted through education allows us to keep a clear focus on what actually happens in schools. Schools are complex organizations and they are hierarchically arranged by the social background of their parent bodies. Thus, a student attending an academically demanding private school and a student placed in a vocational track in a high school located in a poor urban neighborhood may both be high school students, but actually they are undergoing radically different preparations for life. As different as high schools are, however, they share a tripartite curriculum structure.

At the surface level, schools are organized around academic offerings. This is the public face of schools. Students take certain subjects that represent official knowledge, they are graded, and if they graduate they are certified to possess the knowledge of a high school graduate. This is the manifest curriculum.

But, of course, like prisons, schools are largely run by the inmates. In every high school there is a student culture based on popularity, looks, athletic ability, sexual appeal, and teenage coolness (Murray, 2004; see Kerckhoff, 1972, for a typology of high school students that is witty and insightful). This is the latent curriculum. Quite often, student cultures take oppositional stances toward the official academic culture of schools. Teacher's pets, academic grinds, and intellectual and artistically gifted students can be excluded from the world of high school status hierarchies known as cliques. Students of color can be marginalized in predominantly White schools and students whose sexual orientations are not heterosexual can suffer ostracism and sometimes violence. High schools are rough places where the power game gets played out daily.

But underneath the manifest and latent curriculum is an even deeper curriculum. This is a course of study for which there are no books, for which there are no multiple-choice quizzes and there are no official graduation ceremonies. This is the deep structure curriculum that gives emotional substance to class rites of passage and informs students of who has social power and who does not. Exploring the nature of this deep curriculum gives us insight into how class consciousness is structured by schools. The deep curriculum is the sum of the fictional narratives that define the theater of schools. These summative fictional narratives are the internalized stories of students' class experiences and social trajectories. They are the foundational step for becoming a member of a class that is self-consciously aware of its place in the social hierarchy—a class-for-itself.

To accomplish this, our conception of curriculum needs to be expanded to include all aspects of the drama we call school: its physical setting and ascetics, its authority structure, its pedagogic and academic offerings, its influence on how students define themselves as members of a social class, and its power to allocate students to their most likely class communities. All of this constitutes the deep curriculum that works to forge a clear sense of class identity and facilitates class reproduction as a "natural" expression of attending high school. High schools are power systems designed for long-lasting socialization; what students hear, see, feel, and fear shapes their worldviews and sense of the possible.

Reproduction, Not Replication

This brings us to an important point. The historian George Dyson (1997), in discussing the evolution of social intelligence, makes a distinction between reproduction and replication in the development of species. If species simply replicated themselves, there would be no change and no growth. Reproduction allows for anomalies and differences. Reproduction means that while species retain their basic characteristics, they are also capable of adaption. What is true in nature is true in society. Classes do not replicate themselves; they reproduce themselves. This is not just a semantic distinction—it is a real difference. Classes are populated by what can be thought of as modal class actors; not everyone who undergoes a class rite of passage is transformed, but most are. Class reproduction does not require that every individual internalize the values of his or her class. Overly deterministic theories of class reproduction reify the process and pass over resistance and originality.

Schools do not replicate social classes; they reproduce social classes. Every generation has stylistic, cultural, and even ethical differences from the generations before it and from those that will follow it. Not every student who undergoes a class rite of passage is identical to other students, but they do share many fundamental social characteristics. Just as all tigers have stripes but vary in terms of size, aggressiveness, and hunting ability, the graduates of class-based high schools may vary in terms of academic ability, sociability, and ambition, but most are still members of their class.

Class, Race, and Gender

Generally speaking, when Americans think of inequality they think of race and gender as the two primary divisions in social life. And both race and gender play a huge role in the creation and maintenance of the divisions that shape American society. Separating class from race, race from gender, and class from gender in trying to determine how individuals and groups are assigned certain statuses in industrial and postindustrial societies is complex and does not lend itself to easy answers because these divisions overlap with each other and are not always in opposition to each other.

Attempting to sort out the socialization effects of high schools in the context of the complex interplay of class, race, and gender is a formidable intellectual task because by their very nature these characteristics are intertwined and interconnected. At the same time, it is not a challenge to be avoided because class rites of passage undoubtedly vary significantly according to gender and race. It would be surprising if a female African American student experienced the class infusion process in the same way as a White male student, even holding constant academic program and school culture (Cookson & Persell, 1991). Similarly, it would be surprising if an adolescent male from the Dominican Republic underwent the identical rite of passage with a Dominican female even if they attended the same school.

To make matters more complex, gender and race interact with class in significantly different ways. Class position and race are highly correlated. Although some African Americans have been upwardly mobile since the 1960s many, many more have been left behind. Because of residential segregation by income today we are in some ways a more racially divided society than we were 30 years ago. De jure segregation may have ended in 1954, but de facto segregation is very much alive. Most high schools are segregated by race and class; separating class from race in trying to determine the effects of the class rite of passage on students' collective memories requires a discerning research methodology.

The compounding effect of race and class makes it difficult for people of color to cross class lines unless they have outstanding educational advantages or unique talents. Race and class tend to reinforce each other. In *Class Rules*, I make several tentative suggestions of how this process works in each of the five research schools. I make no claims that these observations are definitive or conclusive. But to ignore the effects of race on the formation of collective memory and class reproduction would be a lost opportunity to expand our understanding of the socialization effects of high schools.

Separating gender discrimination and class division requires a nuanced approach to the complexity of how gender and class interact. Although women continue to experience discrimination in the workplace and must struggle for recognition and positions of power, they now comprise more than half of those attending college and own more than 50% of the wealth in the United States. But having said this, the socialization effects of high schools on young women and young men appear to be different. It is still the case that in most high school settings, males attempt to dominate the social if not the academic environment and many high school practices and traditions still elevate masculinity—the cult of football being one example.

It would be very surprising if adolescent girls and adolescent boys experienced the same class rites of passage. It would be equally surprising if the collective memories of high school were the same for both genders. Visiting American high schools, it is obvious that they are highly sexualized environments and that males and females establish somewhat separate cultures within the general school culture. As we will see, this separateness varies by the class composition of the school.

In *Class Rules* we will explore some of these issues from the perspective of the book's thesis. Many of these observations will be tentative; I am not an expert on female socialization and I did not collect enough systematic data to support a full exploration and argument. Nevertheless, to ignore the compelling question of how class rites of passage differently affect females and males would be to ignore an important element in understanding the complexity of class reproduction.

PART TWO: THE SAMPLE SCHOOLS AND ANALYTIC APPROACH

As mentioned in the Introduction, the five representative schools in this study are: Highridge Academy, an upper-class elite private school; Meadowbrook High, a public high school in an upper-middle-class suburb; Riverside High, a public high school in a middle-class neighborhood; Patrick Henry High, a public high school located in a rural working-class town; and Roosevelt High, a public high school in an impoverished inner-city neighborhood.

These schools are arrayed across the class divide according to the social class compositions of their student bodies, histories, and their underlying roles in allocating class position; they are "ideal" types—representing similar schools in their organization, student body composition, and academic programs. With the exception of Meadowbrook, the sample schools are relatively small, with approximately 400 to 600 students. Meadowbrook is a large high school with just less than 2,000 students.

My relation to each of these schools is somewhat different. I have known and studied four of them for many years; one I have come to know more recently. These long-term and in-depth relationships are the foundation of this study. I adapted myself to the environments of the schools and the expectations of their leaders, and I used nonintrusive observational methods for sensitizing myself to the inner life of the schools. My research strategy combined elements of social science with journalism.

Descriptions of class rites of passage are not found in school bulletins, mission statements, or formal curriculum. They are found in the informal interactions of human beings. Although my research strategy might offend some methodological purists, it allowed me to integrate myself into the schools' cultures in a way that enabled me to observe without being disruptive. The less intrusive the investigator, the more likely the findings are to be an expression of the subjects and not the author. Spending time in each of the schools was an essential component of this research. I did not attempt to regulate every aspect of the research so that it was identical for each school. Much depended on the nature of the school culture and the individual participants. I was not seeking to write a study composed of graphs and boxes; this is a study of living interactions.

I have conducted research at Highridge Academy since the 1980s, collecting data and sharing in the academic and cultural life of the school. Elite private schools are not uncharted territory for me (Cookson & Persell, 1985). Meadowbrook High is located near New York City. In 2012, I visited classes, interviewed students, teachers, and administrators, and observed the school's class culture. I have lived near Riverside High since the 1990s, have participated in school activities, and have spent considerable time in the school observing and interacting with students and school personnel. I first became acquainted with Patrick Henry High in the early 1970s and have remained in contact since then. I know the Patrick Henry community well. Roosevelt High is a small school located in what was once a legendary large high school. Since the 1990s I have followed the up and down story of school reform in the South Bronx including the struggles of Roosevelt.

Thus, most of the observational data for this study have been collected over the course of many years. Recent visits to the schools brought my observations up-to-date. In the course of my research I have observed classes and interviewed students, teachers, and administrators. I have collected published data and spent time absorbing the schools' cultures. Many of my strongest impressions came at those unstructured moments when the informal life and class assumptions of the schools were revealed inadvertently.

For instance, I did not undertake this research thinking that differences in what and how much students had to eat would reveal a great deal about the development of class consciousness and play a role in social reproduction. But, after observing the striking differences in how we feed our young adults according to their class backgrounds, I realized how important food is in the social reproductive process. Food, like so much else, is allocated differently by class; the higher the social background of a school's aggregate student body, the healthier and more plentiful the food.

This finding was not isolated. School-based class rites of passage are clearly delineated by a host of organizational features, including cleanliness, safety, and orderliness. You will not find police officers roaming the halls of prep schools as you will in underclass schools, and you will not find middle-class schools short on toilet paper as happens in working-class schools. The latest teenage clothing styles are largely absent in schools that enroll working-class and poor students, but very much in evidence in upper-middle- and upper-class schools. Culture shapes consciousness; understanding culture requires an eye for telling detail and unplanned interaction.

Although the reader will find a good amount of statistical data about each of the schools, the heart and soul of this study is descriptive, even pictorial. The goal of comparative institutional analysis is to separate the forest from the trees; this requires an overarching sense of the schools' unique class culture in which the sum is greater than the parts. My apologies to those researchers who favor less impressionistic techniques. All I can say is that multiple impressions and multiple interactions are a form of knowledge that has a long and esteemed place in the sociological literature and the sociology of education.

I am very skeptical of drama for drama's sake; when we draw negative pictures of schools to titillate, we diminish the good work of educators and students. My research task was not to berate or rate schools but to identify those elements of a school's culture that contribute to class reproduction. Class reproduction is not the result of adversity, but of shared community. It is not pounded into the head, but arises from a "natural" transformation of the head and the heart. I have enormous respect for educators and the work they do, sometimes under very difficult circumstances. My goal is not to make invidious comparisons, but to illuminate those elements of school life that structurally ensure that class inequality is passed from generation to generation.

KEY NARRATIVES IN CLASS RITES OF PASSAGE

Which organizational narratives matter most in the class reproduction process? To answer this question, it is helpful to reconnect with the study's purpose. We are interested in uncovering how class reproduction works in the high school setting. What are the major organizational, academic, and cultural elements of a school that infuses students with class consciousness? I would argue that out of the many institutional practices that describe high schools, there are five main practices or organizational narratives that directly impact the collective social class memories of students. I have chosen these five because they touch on the basic processes of socialization and signal to the outside world a school's social class charter. There might well be others, but these five seem indispensable.

I refer to these organizational practices and pedagogies as narratives because they tell the dramatic story of class reproduction not just in words but also in places, actions, and relationships. I hypothesize that these narratives, taken together, form a matrix in which students come to internalize their class position and socially evolve into class actors capable of joining with others as a class-for-itself. Collective memory does not arise from singular events or random interactions; it arises from a consistent, powerful, and structured set of prescribed experiences. Class rites of passage have been set in place long before individual students arrive at the school's doorstep. Students are confronted with these organizational and cultural practices as new members of a club where the rules have been established and conformity is expected. Each of the five narratives summarized below is treated in depth for each school in its own chapter:

1. *The Architectural/Ascetic Narrative.* When we think of schools, we cannot help but think of them as actual places with buildings, grounds, parking lots, and playing fields. Architecture and ascetics shape consciousness and organize collective memory. Buildings and grounds are powerful transmitters of class messages. Do I go to a school that is beautiful, well equipped, and mirrors back to me a sense of privilege, or do I go to a school that reflects back to me poverty, disorganization, and confusion? Schools physically announce their class position and send unspoken messages to the students who attend them about who they are in the world.

2. *The Authority Narrative.* Who are students' adult role models? A very big part of class socialization is learning whether or not you are a follower, a leader, or a complete outsider. We know from research and experience that the principal is the key role model for students. How does he or she see leadership? What is the underlying message of his or her leadership style? Is it corporate? Is it civil service? Is it the gifted amateur? Is it despotic or democratic? All these different leadership styles teach students different things about the nature of authority and their own prospects of wielding authority.

3. *The Pedagogic/Curriculum Narrative.* Teaching and learning is a political act (Apple, 2004). Learning to critically analyze texts versus filling out workbooks, for example, is not just a difference in pedagogy; it is a difference in preparing for class position. What we learn and how we learn it is based on the class assumptions of parents, teachers, and administrators. From a class reproductive perspective, studying Greek and Latin is qualitatively different from studying woodworking and typing. The word is the world. The more words you have and the more facile you are in using words, the bigger your world. As we will see, pedagogy and curriculum are deeply class-based and form a very important and distinctive role in shaping students' class rites of passage.

4. *The Definition of Self-Narrative.* The most fundamental question an adolescent asks is: Who am I? The second most important question is: Where am I going? Am I going to be a leader? Will I be able to get

into college? Am I going to work at McDonald's after graduation? Does anyone care what happens to me? The answers to these questions are critically important when young people seek to define themselves. Who we are, or more correctly, who we think we are, has a great deal to do with our inner sense of self. Can I get things done? Do I control my own destiny? Am I empowered or disempowered?

Empowerment is a slippery concept because it is used so casually. But it does have meaning. Psychologist Felicia Pratto and her colleagues (1994) explored the importance of empowerment as part of a study of what they call *social dominance orientation*. She and her colleagues argue:

> Ideologies that promote or maintain group inequality are the tools that le-
> gitimate discrimination. To work smoothly, these ideologies must be widely
> accepted within society, appearing as self-evident truths; hence we call them
> hierarchy-legitimating myths. By contributing to consensual or normalized
> group-based inequality, legitimating myths help to stabilize oppression. (p. 741)

The authors conclude that institutional discrimination is one of the major contributors to the creation and maintenance of social inequalities and social hierarchy. As we will see, the higher a school is in the hierarchy of high schools, the more students' rites of passage emphasize social dominance and class empowerment and, in the words of Pratto and her colleagues, stabilize oppression.

An individual's internal self-evaluation about his or her own empowerment and the power of his or her class has a great deal to do with what happens to the individual in life. Although there are many combinations of traits related to feelings of empowerment, there are two that emerge from the literature that have been found to be consistently significant: self-efficacy (Bandura, 1993) and locus of control (Judge & Bono, 2001). Psychologist Albert Bandura (1993) describes the importance of self-efficacy as follows:

> People make causal contributions to their own functioning through mechanisms
> of personal agency. Among the mechanisms of agency, none is more central or
> pervasive than people's beliefs about their capabilities to exercise control over
> their own level of functioning and over events that affect their lives. Efficacy
> beliefs influence how people, feel, think, motivate themselves and behave. Self-
> efficacy beliefs produce these diverse effects through four major processes. They
> include cognitive, motivational, affective and selection processes. (p. 118)

Self-efficacy is an estimate of one's ability to cope, perform, and be successful. A strong sense of self-efficacy is closely related to a sense of agency, which in turn is closely related to feelings of powerfulness and powerlessness. When we feel we can cause events instead of events having control over us, we feel empowered with a strong sense of purpose. Students gain a sense of self-efficacy and agency from their social and school environments (Bandura, 1993). The class-based relationships students form while in school significantly contribute to their sense of agency and empowerment.

Acquiring a sense of agency and feeling empowered also is related to the degree to which individuals and groups look to themselves to shape events or wait for external—sometimes magical—events to shape their lives. Where is my locus of control? Am I the master of my own fate or is my fate written on the stars? Self-evaluation depends heavily on locus of control, according to Judge and Bono (2001). "Internal locus of control was considered a manifestation of core evaluations because internals believe they can control a broad array of factors in their lives" (p. 86). An individual or group with a strong sense of self-efficacy and an internal locus of control is far more likely to feel empowered than an individual or group low on both these characteristics.

Ultimately, the acid test for my argument is evidence that the fictional narratives that constitute the drama of schooling become part of the collective memories of most students attending the high schools studied. We cannot open the brains of the students and observe their thoughts, feelings, and memories, but we can make informed surmises and theoretically founded connections. Assessing the intensity, frequency, and emotional impact of student life is one way of inferring the likelihood that collective memories are being created and internalized.

5. *The Community Narrative.* Who will be my adult peer group? Am I headed to a big job in corporate America or am I headed to a lifetime of marginal employment? Becoming upwardly mobile implies understanding the world of work, who has economic power, and the organization of labor. Learning these lessons is a key narrative in students' rites of passage. Schools vary significantly on the depth and breadth of their social horizons and their ability to transmit the economic nature of advanced capitalism to their students. The larger the horizon, the more room for ambition to grow.

When these five narratives are arrayed against the five social classes we arrive at a five-by-five summary matrix (see Table 1.1). When the matrix is read vertically, it describes the characteristics of each class's rite of passage, and when it is read horizontally, it compares the five narratives by class. For instance, if we read down the upper-class vertical, we see that the upper-class rites of passage are rooted in British/ Ivy league ascetic sensibilities, is most comfortable with top-down but benign authority relationships,

elevates a traditional classical curriculum, assumes that students will be society's leaders, and considers the globe to be home. In other words, the
young upper-class adult is now practically and psychologically prepared to
assume power, the master narrative of his or her class.

What this matrix communicates is that the deep curriculum of class reproduction is extensive and systematic; the pieces of the puzzle fit together.
Thus, for example, the middle-class school rite of passage is cohesive from
its physical setting, to its authority structure, to its teaching and curriculum,
to how students see themselves in the world, and to the community students
are most likely to identify with or aspire to join. Graduates of middle-class
high schools are chartered to be middle-class. They have shared collective
memories and are ready to join with other members of the middle class in
advancing and protecting their class interests. And so it is with the other
class rites of passage. The reproduction process goes on almost unnoticed.
It feels natural and fitting.

CONCLUSION: WHAT CONSTITUTES PROOF?

The next five chapters examine in depth the five class rites of passage. The
form of analysis is comparative and institutional. Comparative institutional
analysis is convincing according to the total weight of evidence it brings to
bear on the argument being made. If the analysis reveals distinct differences
in the school-based rites of passage and if these rites of passage are correlated to class position, we have *prima facia* evidence, which supports this
study's central argument.

I have used the comparative institutional approach in previous research
(Cookson, 1981; Cookson & Embree, 1999; Cookson & Persell, 1985). By
directly comparing schools on a set of common variables, patterns of institutional values and behaviors emerge from which we can draw plausible
inferences. These inferences either support or refute the central arguments
of the study (Etzioni, 1975). The key to this method is discipline in the use
of comparisons; that being the case, each of the chapters is very similar in
structure and the data presented. The comparative institutional approach
keeps the data collection and analysis at the group level and in doing so
allows us to assess the effects of institutional practices across classes. There
is no single proof point in this type of research. There is no smoking-gun
statistic. We are convinced by the accumulation of evidence and the logic
that explains the evidence.

Table 1.1 The Class Rites of Passage Matrix

Narrative	*Upper-Class*	*Upper-Middle-Class*	*Middle-Class*	*Working-Class*	*Underclass*
Architectural/ Ascetic	British or early American	High-concept corporate	Office Recreation center	Functional No frills	Tenement Soft prison
Authority	Benign despot	CEO	Mid-level Professional	Coach	Civil servant
Pedagogic/ Curriculum	Classical Concentrated	Classical Enriched	Traditional Enriched	Traditional Minimal Vocational	Basic Vocational
Definition of Self	Leader	Professional	Mainstream Citizen	Laborer	Estranged from mainstream
Community	Global Social elite	Global corporate Business elite	Regional White-collar	Local Trades and services	Neighborhood Marginal employment

2

The Upper-Class Rite of Passage

SOFT CALVINISM AT YOUR SERVICE

Highridge Academy was founded in the 1890s. Located in a bucolic New England setting, Highridge began with an original bequest of several hundred acres and today the boarding school sits at the center of a manicured 1,000-acre campus. It is among the schools E. Digby Baltzell (1958) identified as serving the "sociological function of differentiating the upper classes from the rest of the population" (p. 293). Tuition, boarding, and fees amount to over $50,000 a year. The school selects its students carefully, measuring academic ability, special talents, and class background.

While most of the nearly 300 American boarding schools are located on the East Coast, there is some variation in terms of size, religious affiliation, geographic location, and educational philosophy, ranging from the very progressive to the very traditional. Academies such as Exeter and Andover were founded in the 18th century to prepare young gentlemen to be leaders in the young republic. Since that time, boarding schools have spread across the country and include the following major types (Cookson & Persell, 1985): academies, Episcopal, entrepreneurial, all-girls, Catholic, western, progressive, military, and Quaker.

Socially elite families founded entrepreneurial schools, like Highridge, in the late 19th century to prepare their sons for lives of power and influence. These schools modeled themselves after English "public" schools such as Eton and Harrow, borrowing English terminology and curricula, such as *headmaster* rather than *principal*, forms rather than grades, and British history rather than American social studies. In many ways, Highridge has all the trimmings of the quintessential entrepreneurial prep school, including a love of sport, a long-lasting relationship to the Ivy League and a permanent connection to wealth.

The school became co-ed in the early 1970s along with many other prep schools; today, the school enrolls approximately 600 students. The official reason for admitting girls was that the school was keeping up with the spirit of the times but another, more pressing, reason was the admissions policies of the most selective colleges and universities were becoming somewhat liberalized and Highridge and other prep schools needed girls' academic brain power. Highridge is somewhat more racially diverse than many other prep schools; today nearly 40% of the students define themselves as students of color—a very high percentage of these students are from Asia or are Asian Americans.

From its inception Highridge has attracted wealthy upper-class families from New York and Boston in part because of its Anglophile traditions and in part because it is a feeder school to Yale and other Ivy League colleges and universities. The list of its alumni reads like a virtual *Who's Who* in 20th-century American history. Its graduates include corporate CEOs, publishers, prize-winning authors and journalists, lawyers and judges (including a Supreme Court justice), politicians and high-level presidential advisors, entrepreneurs, media leaders, and famous academics. Its board of trustees primarily is composed of notable and wealthy alumni; the collective wealth of its graduates is equal to the gross domestic product of a small and successful country.

This aspect of life at Highridge should not be underestimated. Most high schools have some graduates that have gone on to fame and fortune, although not usually because of where they went to high school. Highridge and other elite schools are not just good high schools that happen to have some famous alumni. Elite private schools are key institutions of the American establishment. Although it is true that a great deal of the country's wealth is currently located on the West Coast, Texas, and in parts of the Midwest, it is still the case that most of the concentrated wealth of the United States remains on the East Coast, particularly in New York. The Protestant establishment that Digby Baltzell wrote about in the 1950s and 1960s may have to share some of the power limelight with the new rich, but it still commands center stage.

Highridge is not just a good high school; it is far more: It is a private upper-class institution with its own board of trustees, answerable to the larger public only in the most narrow and legal sense as a tax-exempt organization. Highridge can teach what it wants, when it wants, and to whom it wants. It is a club as well as a school; it is an enclosed world of privilege. Highridge is the gateway to admission to highly selective and socially prestigious colleges and universities, it is a key credential for acceptance into private clubs, and it is a very useful credential when seeking employment in blue chip and socially prestigious firms. It integrates graduates into a network of the privileged, some of whom go on to be society's movers and shakers.

Visiting Highridge is to step into another world. When social observers write about entitlement, it tends to have an edgy flavor—us against them. But for those who are actually entitled, the world is not divided so starkly. Life is good at Highridge. Most students are eager to be successful and save the world at the same time. They are open to conversation and express themselves in complete sentences and developed thoughts. They appreciate art and intellectual achievement. In short, they are on their way to becoming gentlewomen and gentlemen. Their collective memories are based on interactions that center on a shared worldview that is traditional, worldly, and decidedly upper-class.

One hundred percent of Highridge graduates attend college. The most heavily attended colleges and universities in the last 5 years are Harvard, Princeton, Yale, Georgetown, University of Pennsylvania, Middlebury, Dartmouth, Cornell, Bucknell, New York University, Brown, Columbia, Stanford, and Williams. Although admissions policies at Ivy League and near–Ivy League colleges and universities have been somewhat democratized in the last 3 decades, the reality is that Highridge students are highly sought after by socially and academically selective colleges.

Highridge graduates are attractive to admissions officers not only because of their academic preparation, but also because upper-class students do not need scholarships; excel at sports such as crew, hockey, and squash; and they have already demonstrated that they play the school game well. When they graduate, they are likely to have the means to make significant donations to their alma mater. In short, Highridge Academy is an excellent example of a private, socially elite high school that educates youthful members of the upper class and reproduces the upper class with unerring reliability. It is a status seminary where adolescents acquire the attitudes, values, and behaviors of those who are expected to live, work, and play at the commanding heights.

THE UPPER-CLASS RITE OF PASSAGE

The underlying metaphor for the upper-class rite of passage is power. Driving by an elite boarding school might give you the impression of an educational paradise and in some ways it is. The rituals of upper-class infusion, however, are not bucolic; they are closer to fire than water. The deep curriculum at elite schools has been refined over the decades, and because elite boarding schools are able to socialize their students 24 hours a day, they are able to dig deeply into the psyches of their students. The upper-class rite of passage at Highridge and schools like it is a well-traveled path for discovering how power is used by those who possess it in a society that prides itself on its democratic principles.

As students learn to play their parts in the drama of becoming upper-class they are infused with a worldview where might and right are not opposites and where success is the signature of a life well lived. Leadership is the watchword. From the headmaster to the students to the graduates, one hears that attendance at Highridge is preparation for leadership. Students assume that their lives will be in positions of power and influence. They have been chosen. In this sense, they are already a class-for-itself.

The Architectural/Ascetic Narrative

At the end of the 19th century, the American upper class fell in love with all things British. The feeling was mutual. Men of the British upper class, desperate for money, married wealthy American women in the futile hope of holding on to their huge estates. This mutual reinforcement process created an Anglo-American upper crust and upper class. The *Social Register* was founded to ensure that bloodlines are traceable to socially "correct" stock. It is not surprising, then, that American boarding schools borrowed a great deal from elite British public schools not only educationally, but also ascetically. This cultural borrowing is reflected in the architecture and ascetics of Highridge; the love of cultivated and refined nature, the choice of classical architectural design, and the expansive green lawns that serve as playing fields all emulate the taste of the British upper class.

Highridge is a small, well-appointed, and immaculately kept village, complete with a golf course, a farm, wetlands, lakes, a chapel, a huge sports complex, colonial-style academic buildings and residences halls, a power plant, kitchens, laundries, and acres and acres of playing fields. Entering the school, the visitor passes through an impressive ivy-covered brick gate that opens up to a long tree-lined driveway sweeping toward the horizon and ends at the marble steps of the main building. The school has been built in stages, starting with a central building, which is definitely "old school," complete with wood paneling and floor-to-ceiling glass cases bulging with trophies won in athletic victory over other prep schools.

Prep school athletic rivalries are very old, very fierce, and very important to many graduates. The school head under whose watch the home team loses more than once or twice to a traditional rival may find that his or her tenure is shorter than he or she expected. Complementing this traditional prep love of athletic display, the great hall leading to the headmaster's office is lined with well-broken-in leather couches and armchairs, tasteful lamps that cast a warm light, and oversized tables artfully littered with old books and school literature. Oil paintings, old and modern, are hung together in an understated display of high culture.

Fanning out from the central building is the rest of the academic village; immaculate and freshly painted buildings are connected to each other by well-tended gray gravel walkways. Flower beds edge the walkways, highlighting a sense of beauty and ease. Well-cultivated shrubbery, benches, and an occasional sundial grace quads and quiet places. Tasteful modern sculpture, placed in key intersections and vistas, signal to the knowing world the refined taste of a class that can afford to collect expensive art. The neatly trimmed lawns are uninterrupted by weeds or crab grass; large majestic oak and maple trees signal that Highridge was not born yesterday.

One of the signature characteristics of the upper class is its insistence on taste. Taste implies refinement; refinement implies leisure; leisure implies enough unearned income to live well without working; not having to work implies not having to get "one's hands dirty," to use an old but telling phrase. Upper-class tastefulness is hard to define because it often emphasizes less rather than more and display is subtle rather than overt; upper-class taste is about understatement and countersnobbery. Gross overt displays of wealth are frowned upon. The ascetics at Highridge signal an assured sense of taste that emphasizes refinement and elegance—not the usual adjectives one associates with high schools.

Food is abundant, tasty, and healthy. Students and faculty eat their meals in a huge dining hall that is more than a little Harry Potteresque, complete with gothic statues, flags from around the world, and long tables for collective feeding. There are few lines at the multiple salad bars and seconds—and thirds—are always available. Students have a variety of hot dishes to choose from on a daily basis that might include beef stroganoff, several pasta offerings, and fresh fish. These entrees are prepared by experienced chefs and their assistants; quality matters and the "feed," to use the British term, is an important part of school life. Breakfast at Highridge is plentiful, including eggs, pancakes, sausage, bacon, potatoes, and fresh fruit. All of this is managed by a school staff that works seamlessly behind the scenes in true upstairs/downstairs fashion. Privilege is not something to be ashamed of; it is something to celebrate.

The deep curriculum of class privilege and power at Highridge is chiseled into the very institutional soul of the school. Exclusiveness sends a message to the students at Highridge: They are part of an international set that lives well and has access to the best things in life; ordinary people are there to make them comfortable and, if they don't mess up, they are protected from the rough-and-tumble of the workaday world. Highridge students are part of an Anglo-American world that has deep traditions and represents the "best" culture has to offer. The architectural/ascetic narrative of Highridge is clear: This is where power emanates. Life at the top is good.

The Authority Narrative

The head of Highridge is an experienced leader in the independent school world. His perspective is international; he was hired by the schools' trustees in part because of his forward-thinking global philosophy of education tempered, of course, with a firm understanding of the school's central so-cializing mission. Tall, lanky, and looking just a little bit like Gary Cooper, the head of Highridge is thoughtful, mildly ironic, kind and considerate, all wrapped around a will of steel—the iron fist in the velvet glove (see Cookson & Persell, 1985, for a full description of the characteristics of elite school heads).

Unlike public school principals who must acquire state certifications to become school leaders, there are no formal or state credentials to be the head of an elite private school. In fact, graduating from a college of edu-cation or possessing a state administrative certificate would be considered a barrier to being hired as a head because, rather than signaling executive preparation, paper credentials suggest a careerism that is far from the am-ateur ideal that is at the heart of the upper-class leadership style. The best credential to have for the aspiring young head is a bachelor's degree with honors in British history from an Ivy League college or university or, even better, from Oxford or Cambridge University in the United Kingdom.

When choosing a head to run their school, trustees are partial to some-one who is like them in style and class background. Until the 1980s, all heads at the boys' schools were male. Today, there are several female heads of co-ed elite schools. On the face of it, this might appear to be a cultural breakthrough, but class unity almost always trumps gender divisions. It is not surprising, therefore, that male and female heads may differ slightly in their leadership styles, but not on the fundamentals of class reproduction.

Nearly all elite school heads are from upper-class or upper-middle-class backgrounds. They often start as teachers in elite schools; very, very few begin their careers in public schools. Crossing the private/public boundary is difficult, if not impossible. There is no formal career path to a headship, but there are some key moves that an ambitious teacher ought to take if she or he wants to rise in the private school world. It helps to be an all-around amateur scholar and athlete, loyal, and a sophisticated advocate for the enlightened leadership of the upper class.

Elite school heads represent an Old World model of leadership where charisma, subtly, and an easy self-confidence matters. Authority is exercised with a light but firm touch. School heads do not yell, do not carry clipboards, and do not tolerate rudeness. Although they report to a board of trustees and must maintain positive relationships with parents, elite school heads are relatively autonomous in how they run their school. They are one of the last educational CEOs who can successfully operate as benign despots.

Upper-class leaders rule by indirection and inference. But underneath the self-deprecating exterior is a deeply resolute self. Fairness, or at least the appearance of fairness, is the best defense against accusations of unearned privilege and power. At Highridge, the head is a charming, cultured man of the world, comfortable in the classroom and the drawing room. He has a gentle sense of humor, but this gentleness should not be interpreted as weakness. He is quite steely, determined, and not easily deceived—a near-perfect upper-class leadership role model.

The Pedagogic/Curriculum Narrative

Academically, Highridge is very rigorous; there is tremendous pressure on Highridge students to be academically and socially successful. As mentioned above, the theme of leadership is a leitmotif of the school's daily life; the school's mission statement emphasizes the need for graduates to assume stewardship roles in the world. The schools' educational philosophy emphasizes mastery of academic skills and the development of curiosity, creativity, and responsibility. With more than 15 departments, the school offers students learning opportunities that are sophisticated and varied. The core curriculum is classical and traditional, focusing on English, mathematics, science, foreign language, history, and the arts.

The Highridge curriculum, however, is far more varied and sophisticated than an adequate high school curriculum: Students can take 4 years of Greek, Latin, and Chinese as well as other modern languages. Every department offers required courses but also offers electives such as creative writing; literary criticism; studies in culture; applied scientific research; a full array of theater, art, music, and dance courses; micro- and macroeconomics; and interdisciplinary courses. Highridge prides itself on its global curriculum and its commitment to environmental sustainability. In all, the school offers more than 250 courses. The faculty-to-student ratio is 1:5, allowing for individualized teaching and learning.

There are more than 30 classrooms and labs at the school, all of which contain the newest technology and views overlooking the schools' rolling green fields and grounds. All students have computers and the school has a state-of-the-art computer center. The library is over 20,000 square feet with more than 200 carrels and 20 computer workstations. A member of an international consortium of libraries, the library at Highridge has access to 50 million books, articles, and abstracts. The science building includes an electron microscope and a weather station, and the art and performance facilities include a 700-person concert hall, a proscenium theater, five art studios, five dark rooms, and a screening room. It should be added that Highridge is not unique in the richness of its academic offerings among the select 16 schools—there are some elite schools that have a more expansive and challenging curricula.

Highridge has expanded its curriculum in the last 30 years. There are interdisciplinary studies, internships, programs abroad, and expanded science programs. Yet, the elite schools are far from "shopping-mall" high schools. Students are exposed to a concentrated classical curriculum that emphasizes depth of study and the mastery of basic communication skills such as writing. This cultural capital acquisition is an essential component of the upper-class rite of passage because in an age when apparel has been democratized and popular culture determines the taste patterns of many Americans, sophisticated and nuanced communication skills are one of the signifiers of class position.

On average, the nearly 150 faculty members at the school have 18 or more years of teaching experience. The overwhelming majority of faculty lives on campus and nearly all faculty members serve as athletic coaches, mentors, and residence hall advisors/surrogate parents/rule enforcers. Teachers at Highridge and other elite schools are hired for their cultural compatibility rather than their state credentials. Most teachers have graduated from private, highly selective colleges or universities; many hold advanced degrees from internationally recognized research universities. Many teachers have attended boarding schools or other elite private schools and all have mastered the cultural codes of the upper class; otherwise they would not last long.

Classes are small at Highridge so that the teacher–student relationship is not at arm's length; elite schools developed the concept of individual learning before the phrase was coined in the jargon of educational reform. There is no escape from the watchful eyes of teachers at Highridge, and there is no escape from study. Although the teaching styles at Highridge have softened from the "stand and deliver" days, teachers at Highridge remain authority figures. From a social class infusion perspective, teachers are the primary human mechanism by which the deep curriculum is internalized by students.

Teachers are on the front lines of suppressing possible student opposition. The pedagogic/curriculum narrative of elite schools is meant to channel student resistance, ambivalence, and occasional rebellion into a precut riverbed of class reproduction—and teachers are in charge of steering the riverboat of class reproduction through the rough rapids of adolescence. In talking with teachers, it is clear that a major part of their job is to ensure that students are not only academically prepared but also socially prepared. For some teachers, this part of their mission is gladly embraced; for others it feels a little like an imposition. But in the end, everyone must embrace the school's mission; otherwise the deep curriculum might be implemented in a half-hearted way that would undermine the school's purpose.

As mentioned earlier, prep schools emphasize sports: In fact, most prep schools are sports crazy. Nearly every student is on a team and competition between prep schools is fierce. Major prep schools feed athletes to Ivy League and eastern liberal arts colleges in such sports as crew, ice hockey, lacrosse, tennis, field hockey, squash, and golf. Prep schools do not play public schools in sports for two reasons: One, class mixing can lead to trouble, and two, they most certainly would lose, and, thus, the bubble of prowess and excellence could be broken. There is one sport, however, that Highridge and other prep schools can compete with and beat the best public schools and small colleges—ice hockey. Highridge has a huge ice hockey facility and imports players from Canada regularly. Goalies are in high demand. Elite boarding schools compete with each other not only on the ice but over the ice—nearly all prep schools have hockey facilities that are new, enormous, flashy, professional, and well equipped.

In some ways, the pedagogic/curriculum narrative is the lynchpin in the upper-class rite of passage, providing an intellectual scaffolding that justifies the maintenance of privilege under the mantle of academic excellence. Students come to believe in themselves and their class because they are in possession of the higher learning, which is rewarded by admittance to the best colleges and universities. This sense of superiority, however, does come with an emotional price tag and a required set of social blinders.

The Definition of Self-Narrative

Amanda attended a well-known country day school in New England before enrolling in Highridge Academy. Her father is a partner in a prestigious Wall Street brokerage firm his grandfather founded and her mother is a physician, practicing at a major hospital. Amanda is under a great deal of pressure to be successful because it is a family tradition; if she fails to get into Harvard, Yale, or Princeton, she will consider herself a failure. Amanda is captain of the girls' hockey team, sings in the school's glee club, is member of the French club, tutors special education students at a nearby public school, and is a member of the choir.

She worries she isn't doing enough. She has little trouble accepting the school's demanding honor code, but she worries that her social life and spirituality are suffering. She has many friends at school but keeps her innermost thoughts to herself. She texts and tweets her friends and has a Facebook page but by no means considers herself a techie.

Amanda tries to reconcile the school's call for service with her parents' demand for success. She must give up parts of herself to be accepted in the prep school world, but tries in small ways to resist the upper-class rite of passage, knowing in the end she will conform—her future depends on it and her social class standing requires it. Very little is left to chance at Highridge; the faculty and administration are vigilant in enforcing rules, ensuring that students fit in, and guiding the transformation process. But socialization, like repression, sometimes comes at a cost—a partial loss of self.

Amanda's story is not atypical. She must negotiate the hothouse atmosphere of the upper-class status seminary. Excellence is expected. Status matters. Athletic prowess, good looks, poise, and enough money to spend on vacations to Europe are solid markers of status. This pressure creates a strong student subculture that runs counter to the professed public goals of the school, but merges easily with the unstated goals of the deep curriculum. Most students know that the upper-class rite of passage is really about power, and they establish demanding and at times demeaning student hierarchies where power is exercised on a daily basis.

Students rate and berate each other over a myriad of criteria from how they dress, to whom they date, to verbal cleverness, to who is most likely to succeed. All of this competition is expressed in a special prep style that is at once aristocratic and slightly anarchistic in a stylist way. Lisa Birnbach and Chip Kidd (2010), in authentic tongue-in-cheek prep style, capture this special cultural flavor in their book, *True Prep: It's a Whole New Old World*. This is their version of the prep "manifesto":

> It's about ease and confidence. It's about fitting in when you do and even when you don't. It's about your endless supply of clothes that always look the same, no matter what the era or fashion dictates. It's about your ability to tell a story, be the fourth—for tennis or bridge—or somehow come to the rescue of a social situation. Because you can. Because your parents taught you by example. Maybe you attended an historic prep school. Maybe you didn't. Of course, it's better if you did because then you've been acculturated. You may protest, but you know some literature, know some history, know some sportsmanship, and know that a tie will do when you can't find your belt. (p. 3)

Funny, but true. The upper-class rite of passage requires that students forgo a great deal of individuality and accept a great deal that is ritualistic and, to the outsider, might seem ridiculous. Preparing for power is not for the faint-hearted. Becoming a full-fledged member of the upper class entails the sacrifice of some significant parts of the self and a willingness to live the values associated with privilege: service, the exercise of power, and an exclusiveness that is generally camouflaged by understatement. Hence, the importance of countersnobberies such as old cars, old shoes, old family ties, and of course, old money. There is enormous pressure on Highridge students to fit in; understanding the codes and cues of class equate to fitting in. It isn't just a matter of culture; it's a form of social dominance.

For students of color, this tight and exclusive culture can be emotionally and socially trying. Students of color quite often keep to themselves, eat at their own table during the feed, and generally try to maneuver the tightrope stretched between the African American world and the upper-class

Anglo-American world. Many minority students are on scholarship. They are the outsiders-within. They benefit from the upper-class rite of passage because they are turbo-charged in the college admissions game, but they are also burdened with the understanding that they are very unlikely to be fully accepted into the upper-class world.

For affluent girls undergoing the upper-class rite of passage, the challenges are somewhat different. Like Amanda, they are well schooled to become successful. The pressure put on these young women is considerable. Perfection is a high bar. Competing with other girls and boys who relish competition and are pushed to succeed by their parents leaves little room for individuality or creativity. The pressure is intense and failure is always a possibility. Suicide is not unknown in the elite schools, and depression is common. There is one best way in the elite schools; the maintenance of the upper-class image and self-image is a full-time job.

Boarding school students cannot escape the total institution. The schools were established for the purpose of transforming young people into upper-class adults. Men and women who have attended boarding schools have powerful, sometimes searing, memories of the time they spent in the classrooms, dorms, dining halls, and on the playing fields. Graduates tend to stay in touch, often marry, join the same professions and social clubs, and return regularly to their school for alumni events. They are part of a special community that is highly prestigious and at the same time comfortable. They are part of a national and international network that is personally and professionally embracing.

Memories are powerful, clear, and emotionally relevant to the present; in terms of intensity, frequency, and emotional impact the years spent at boarding school are a major element in a graduate's autobiography. Prep school graduates share a collective identity based on shared experience and repetitive encounters. This collective identity is the foundation for class consciousness and class formation. They internalize the values, dispositions, and beliefs of their class and are well on their way to becoming a class-for-itself.

The upper-class rite of passage builds self-confidence and a positive self-image, which is closely related to a positive sense of self-efficacy. Who am I? Do I shape the future or am I just a passenger in history? From the moment students at Highridge and other elite schools enter school, they are told they must be successful. This message is reinforced by the illustrious graduates of the school who often return to share war stories and to encourage the next generation to take its rightful place as leaders at the commanding heights. It is also reinforced by the head, who uses nearly every opportunity to tell the students—and their parents—that the fate of the earth hangs on the leadership abilities of the graduates of Highridge.

The upper class imagines it is destined to lead; students at Highridge are not being trained to follow. From a chartering perspective this message is dispositive.

Students at Highridge are infused with the success message virtually around the clock. Success often means giving up significant parts of the self. The upper-class rite of passage means the acquisition of those personal qualities needed to exercise power—self-discipline, self-promotion, and self-confidence. From an institutional perspective, the upper-class rite of passage is designed to educate adolescents for power and for feeling empowered. Upper-class students are subjected to a socialization process that consistently and persistently reinforces the message that they have the ability to cope, perform, and be successful. They are expected to function at the high end of the self-efficacy continuum. Through a class infusion experience that includes sticks, carrots, and sermons (early and often), upper-class students pass through a rite of passage that is designed to build self-confidence and a sense of empowerment.

In terms of locus of control, the upper-class rite of passage does not encourage rescue fantasies, magical thinking, or seeking external explanations for naturally occurring events. What the readers of *True Prep* may not fully realize is that underneath the silliness beats the heart of a diluted but still proud and hardheaded Calvinism. The French 16th-century Protestant theologian John Calvin espoused a complex view of human destiny. On the one hand, people were predestined by God to be saved and there wasn't much individuals could do about it; on the other hand, individuals are absolutely required to obey all the commandments found in the New Testament and live a life of faith. This sense of being the elect, but still having to prove one's worth, has been softened since the first Calvinists arrived in New England, but it has not disappeared. It is the underlying, nearly hidden, basis for the upper-class rite of passage. You are responsible for yourself, even if you do wear plaid Bermuda shorts. Your locus of control is Calvinistic and very much internalized.

The upper-class rite of passage is designed to infuse students with the belief that the future is theirs; they are masters of their own fate, but they are also masters of other people's fate. They are very much a class-for-itself and the keepers of the most exclusive kind of British/American cultural capital. The intense socialization of elite schools emphasizes excellence, responsibility, and service and is organized to produce young men and women who look inside themselves for revelation and reason, not in the stars.

The master narrative of power is focused on the control of this world and not letting others control it. Although some elite school teachers and heads may consult their astrology charts before making decisions, my guess is there are very few and those few keep their wishing close to their chests. Being in control of one's self and others is a signature of upper-class status—whatever the cost. Sentimentality and self-pity are for others. To be upper-class is to be in command. In the birth lottery they have won and there is little motivation to change the rules of the game.

The Community Narrative

Today more than ever, there is an international super upper class (Faux, 2006; Rothkopf, 2008). The upper classes in different countries feel more at home with each other than they do with the citizens of their own countries. This trend has been facilitated and expedited by international travel, international taste patterns, and international business. Many upper-class families have multiple homes and travel almost continuously. Upper-class children and young adults feel quite at home in the world because they have grown up with international experience and many of them know powerful individuals and families on a first-name basis.

The students who attend Highridge and other elite schools assume their community is the world. It is their playground, their network, and their home away from home. This sense of global leadership has enormous ramifications for the students of Highridge because in a world where social and economic success depends on mastering a global environment, the upper class has several built-in advantages—an international perspective, an international network, and an international bank account. The graduates of Highridge are prepared to assume international leadership and much of what happens to them after graduation reinforces this perception.

CONCLUSION:
INSTITUTIONAL IMPACT AND COLLECTIVE MEMORY

Recently, Caroline Persell and I published a chapter highlighting the most recent research on elite schools (Cookson & Persell, 2010). We wanted to know what had changed in the prep school world since *Preparing for Power* was published in the 1980s. In addition to reviewing the literature, I was in the process of collecting data for this book. We began by noting that change comes slowly to prep schools. Despite dramatic innovation and transformation in the world since the mid-1980s, particularly with the explosion of the World Wide Web, we observed:

> While it may be more difficult for the elite to cloister itself, by no means are these schools taking their socialization responsibilities any less lightly; in fact,

such ready scrutiny may even require them to redouble their efforts, often in subtle ways. Recent ethnographies of elite boarding schools suggest that the schools remain as cloistered and "bubble-like" as ever. (p. 15)

We concluded

The deep socialization that we identified twenty-five years ago has not ended or even weakened; times may change, but the preparation for power remains a core mission of the schools. (p. 27)

The institutional impact of attending an elite school is profound. It is similar to a conversion experience. Nearly all prep school graduates can recall their days at school with startling clarity. The five narratives described in this chapter all flow into one another to form an upper-class master narrative about power, how to acquire it, how to use it, and how to keep it. As we have seen, the infusion of these upper-class collective memories can be bittersweet. Students like Amanda must give up parts of themselves in order to fit in. To learn, in sociologist Stanley Aronowitz's terminology, the rules of inclusion and exclusion, is to let go of innocence and adopt a kind of hip cynicism that is worn with a pridefulness that barely covers the unvarnished truth—power comes at a high cost, to those who possess it and to those who don't.

3

The Upper-Middle-Class
Rite of Passage

THE MAKING OF THE MARKETPLACE SELF

Imagine visiting a high school in an affluent neighborhood in Westchester County, New York, or Grosse Point, Michigan, or Marin County, California. What are you likely to see? You might notice that, unlike the Anglophile settings of prep schools, most public high schools serving the upper middle class look much like well-appointed office buildings—attractively, if predictably, functional. There is an unspoken atmosphere of social assurance, self-confidence, and an unabashed desire for material success. On the right hand of the parking lot rest the new, often foreign-made, cars of the students; on the left side are the secondhand and decidedly American-made cars of the faculty. Welcome to upper-middle-class America; welcome to Meadowbrook High.

Meadowbrook is located in one of the most affluent communities in the United States. Less than an hour's commute outside New York City, the Meadowbrook community is the home of millionaire and billionaire bankers, stockbrokers, and hedge fund managers. Over 90% of the town's population is White; 5% is Asian. Less than 2% is African American. The individual annual median income is well above $100,000, but this amount is deceptively low—it is hard to make ends meet on less than $300,000 in a community where a wedding can cost a million dollars and daily transportation is a luxury third car costing over $75,000. *CNN/Money* and *Money Magazine* rate the town as one of the best places to live in the United States; the median cost of a single-family home is just under $2 million and according to state assessors the residential and commercial tax base to support public education is just under half a million dollars per pupil. The average yearly per pupil expenditure hovers around $18,000.

Ascetically, the town is noted for its classical architecture and tree-lined streets. Founded at the end of the 17th century, the town is rich in tradition. Near its center is a graceful Episcopal church that has room for nearly 800 parishioners. Downtown is home for many high-end retailers; fashion is important and social life is intense and competitive. Lavish parties highlight the social season where members of the economic and social "A list" set the cultural tone and act as social gatekeepers. The town's exclusive country clubs and yacht clubs are decidedly private. Nearly everyone who is someone owns a second and even a third home in Aspen or Vail, Colorado, West Palm Beach, or East Hampton.

This is a community in which education is a primary tool for financial and social success and continued upward mobility. As I walk down Main Street it is easy to spot Mercedes, BMWs, and Land Rovers graced with the window decals of illustrious colleges and universities such as Harvard, Yale, and Princeton. In conversations, the question of where you went to school inevitably crops up. In a country that is struggling to provide minimal education for much of its population, the citizens living in this pocket of America are more interested in parsing the educational landscape in search of status and distinction.

Currently, Meadowbrook High enrolls nearly 2,000 students and graduates more than 500 seniors every year. The campus includes a sizable student center, a media center, and many modern labs and classrooms. Over 90% of its teachers have advanced degrees. The school has more than 40 varsity teams with long traditions of winning. Over 80% of Meadowbrook's graduates attend a 4-year college immediately after graduation; another 15% attends 2-year colleges.

Although the range of colleges attended by Meadowbrook graduates is broader than that of the graduates of Highridge, Meadowbrook's placements are impressive. Among the top placements are Harvard, Yale, Georgetown, Cornell, Boston College, New York University, Duke, Princeton, Columbia, Dartmouth, Tufts, the United States Military Academy, Williams, the University of Chicago, the University of Pennsylvania, the University of Connecticut, Carnegie-Mellon, and Bucknell.

The underlying metaphor for the upper middle class is professional status and financial prosperity (Demerath, 2009). The upper middle class is that part of the American class structure that is happily successful and increasingly self-confident. What are the key elements of this self-confidence and sense of efficacy? What are the strands that weave together the upper-middle-class master narrative of prosperity and professionalism?

THE UPPER-MIDDLE-CLASS RITE OF PASSAGE

Affluence is more than a measure of how much you are worth; it is a way of life, a way of thinking, and a way of constructing the self. The culture of affluence holds a fascination for many Americans because the media tends to glorify material wealth over intellectual or spiritual wealth and because we are an acquisitive people. Becoming wealthy is the American Dream. A lifetime of material accumulation might not seem inspiring to some, but to most Americans it does seem like a life well spent. Learning how to market the self and successfully pursue prosperity does not create existential angst in most upper-middle-class men and women who see no harm in accumulating capital and living well. There are few Calvinists, soft or otherwise, sweating out the theological implications of having it all in America's wealthy enclaves.

The Architectural/Ascetic Narrative

Unlike many public school districts, Meadowbrook's school district is steeped in history; the first schoolhouse was built by settlers in the middle of the 17th century. Since that time, there has been a succession of expansions, reorganizations, and acquisitions until today Meadowbrook High sits on over 50 acres of fields, parking lots, and woods. Surrounding the school are very large homes complete with gardens, pools, and tennis courts. The landscaping of the Meadowbrook community reminds one that *House and Garden* may not speak to most of America, but it does have an affluent market that invests heavily in their homes, making them into mini-estates full of imaginative details and inviting places to walk, be seen, and swim.

The school itself is huge and impressive. It announces to the world: *I am here, I am impressive, and I am successful.* There is a sense of order and ingrained organization; every morning the town police department shows up to direct traffic alongside the school's security team because traffic control is no small job; the train of Land Rovers and expensive German cars dropping off students stretches down the block. I am directed to an assigned parking space by a security guard who has been notified to keep an eye out for me. People in the community are in a hurry. Parents and students have their cell phones on and at the ready; there are last-minute discussions between moms or maids and students about afterschool activities. There is a sense of urgency because this is a culture where the concept *time is money* is more than a cliché; it's a way of life. There are no dads to be seen. The security guard accompanies me to the principal's office, where I am greeted, issued a name tag, and take a seat next to a table with several copies of the day's *New York Times*.

Much of the school has glass walls and 20-foot ceilings so that the halls are bright with natural light and with the excellent and colorful artwork of the students. There are numerous trophy cases and banners announcing athletic triumphs. Meadowbrook is a sports powerhouse. Its teams make the local news and state championships are a regular occurrence. The school's many playing fields are in use from dawn to dusk with varsity and JV teams. Many students hire personal trainers to help them develop their athletic talents. Many of the wealthy families who send their children to Meadowbrook are also into fitness and conditioning; health and excellent body image are central to a life spent in the pursuit of status and wealth.

At the center of the school is a very large student center that acts as the school's hub. During class changes it is flooded with students dressed in designer clothes talking, laughing, and flirting. The place buzzes with sociability. Huge flags from faraway places and school club banners adorn the walls and crossbeams. There are small but distinct posters placed in strategic places warning students about using proper language and dressing appropriately—no one, however, except the researcher, is looking at them. Whatever is the definition of appropriate dress, it is apparent that most of the students have their own interpretations: Most boys seem to prefer the rap star look, and many girls choose the movie star on vacation look. Modesty isn't cool.

There is a well-provisioned cafeteria offering healthy salads and a variety of meal options. Unlike many other public school students, the students at Meadowbrook have a choice of meals to suit their taste. Although not as elaborate as the dining facilities at Highridge, the dining opportunities at Meadowbrook are plentiful and healthy. Since most Meadowbrook students are unlikely to go hungry anytime soon, there is little sense of urgency about eating. But as with kids everywhere pizza is a staple.

From this bustling hub, students rush like commuters racing to a train to their classrooms, located down numerous wide hallways. These hallways are really major arteries for the social life of the school: Students have their lockers there, students set up tables for the causes they believe in, and students stop to talk and gossip with each other. As far as I know, there are no studies about gossip in schools, but there should be. Gossip is the lifeblood of schools; it is the major source of information. Gossip is the way students (and teachers) learn about what is hot and what is not, who is seeing whom, who is a good teacher and who is not, and what Jack and/or Mary did or did not do last night. Learning how to gossip well is a social skill that is particularly useful in the office world. Offices run on gossip, and most of Meadowbrook's graduates are headed to careers in offices where they will rise or fall, in part, on the value of the gossip they can share with colleagues and superiors. Almost no one gossips with people who are below them in the class hierarchy.

Once the students get to their classrooms, they find an inviting educational environment, equipped with the latest technology, including a Smartboard, access to the Internet, and comfortable seating. Students are encouraged to use their laptops, although the school blocks some websites. The classrooms are clean, freshly painted, and well lit. Teachers decorate their classrooms with books, inspirational posters, and small mementos of their college days such as a worn football or a college banner. Most of the teachers have graduated from private colleges and universities; there is a subliminal message that educational routes do, indeed, matter.

The school is well equipped; the science wing is better equipped than some small colleges, with many of its classrooms housing the latest scientific equipment, aquariums, dark rooms, computers, and enough space to conduct experiments. Being able to move around a classroom in comfort might not seem that unusual, but in many American schools students are crammed together and teachers have little or no room to work. In some classes, students are issued specially programmed laptops to do their homework, sending their work to their teacher for review.

In general, the facilities are new, well maintained, and modern. The school has several theaters, art studios, and music rooms. Many faculty members have their own offices, which is a luxury that most high schools cannot afford. There is a feeling of professionalism and respect for teachers that is reflected in their professional surroundings. Meadowbrook has a very large administrative staff that works in well-lit, well-equipped, corporate-style office spaces and cubicles. Members of the school staff are expected to be role models to the students, demonstrating what it means to work in a well-run organization. The school has a full-time nurse and several examination rooms.

The Authority Narrative

The principal of Meadowbrook is an education professional with an advanced degree in educational administration from a nationally recognized university. He is thoughtful and organized and radiates calm control; he runs a tight ship. He is not worldly and European in the same way as the head of Highridge; he is very much a typical American educator in his worldview and attitude toward learning. He believes in equality of educational opportunity, even if he knows it doesn't exist in the real world. He is caught between the demands of the state for accountability and standards and his belief in educating the "whole student." Because he shares a great deal in common with Meadowbrook's parent body, he is able to walk the tightrope between the state and the parents who want a private school–type education for their children. His job requires tact, poise, and political savvy when dealing with the state, although it is made easier due to the fact that the Meadowbrook community is wealthy, politically connected, and has little use for civil servants. Nobody who is anybody in the Meadowbrook community works for the state unless he or she is the governor. He knows if he gets on the wrong side of the parent body he will fall off the tightrope, and there is no safety net. And, of course, Meadowbrook meets the standards without even trying because of its wealth of offerings and the background of its student body. Meadowbrook is insulated from the school wars that rage in poorer, weaker communities.

The principal's office is spacious, orderly, and immaculate. The centerpiece is a large American flag. A polished wood meeting table is framed by a circular corner of the office with large windows overlooking the entrance to the school and the driveway. From here, the principal has a commanding view. Unlike the ideal elite school head who is meant to be an inspired idealist with a slight poetic streak, the Meadowbrook principal is a determined executive who believes poetry is best left in the classroom. He is experienced, professionally trained, and promotes efficiency and accountability. He is in charge of a multimillion-dollar operation and reports to a school board composed mostly of successful business and financial executives. The principal must manage a very large staff: There are more than 250 teachers under his supervision and a very large administrative staff. As a role model, he personifies the in-charge executive with polished political skills and a dedication to making the trains run on time. In the leadership literature the distinction is often made between transactional and transformative leadership, but there is another type of leadership between transactional and transformational—intentional. Everything that is done is done for an organizational purpose.

Teachers are evaluated systematically from a variety of perspectives; newsletters are sent to parents regularly; curriculum objectives are considered thoughtfully; discipline is handled by the book, but compassionately; and parents are treated with respect. But the principal is no pushover; he deals with fathers and mothers who are used to getting their way—any sign of weakness on his part is an invitation to a shark attack.

Change is not feared so much as managed; new ideas in education are weighed carefully, researched, and adopted slowly, if at all. The educational silver bullets so loved by the policy world never get a hearing at Meadowbrook. Experimentation for experiment's sake is bad for business and bad for education. All this activity takes place in an atmosphere of rationality and political sensitivity. The principal does not carry a clipboard or bully students in any way; he treats them as young adults in need of some gentle direction. Because authority appears rational and is culturally consistent, it is seldom questioned. It is a lesson that will serve many Meadowbrook students well in their careers. As students undergo the upper-middle-class rite of passage, they learn that authority is a good thing and an even better thing to possess.

The Pedagogic/ Curriculum Narrative

The curriculum at Meadowbrook is deep and broad. Not only is there a full array of core courses, there is a wide selection of electives. But a paper overview of Meadowbrook's curriculum does not really do it justice. Class size at Meadowbrook is roughly 20. As mentioned earlier, classrooms are equipped with many teaching tools, including computers and Smartboards. iPads are regularly used and there is room for some teacher-led experimentation and innovation, although the administration is vigilant in visiting classes and giving teachers feedback in the form of evaluations. The days of sitting in rows and listening to teachers talk are past. There is a lively schoolwide discussion about how to incorporate the newest communication technologies into instruction without losing the intellectual scaffolding that leads to learning. There is a sense of order: no slamming doors, no yelling in the hallways, and students can use the bathrooms when they need them.

Integrated and interdisciplinary classes are increasingly replacing traditional disciplines and chalk-and-talk classes. Students are encouraged to be creative and analytic. Most teachers have ascribed to the *guide on the side* model rather than the *sage on the stage* model. The teaching staff reflects the students demographically and educationally. They are happy to teach at Meadowbrook and they extend themselves to students. Students are encouraged to offer their opinions on nearly all subjects—which they do freely. They are an unusually verbal and an often informed group of students.

The school's vision of a graduate is intellectually demanding, including the ability to ask important questions, organize information, address difficult problems, think of creative solutions, collaborate with others, and develop a desire to keep learning. In many ways, the Meadowbrook curriculum is more enriched and extensive than the curricula at prep schools, including Highridge. The school offers more than 300 courses. The required courses include: 4 years of English and physical education; 3 years of social studies, mathematics, and science, and 1.5 years of art. Students must also pass the standardized tests required by the state. The curriculum is enriched with individual learning opportunities. The English curriculum, for example, offers courses in British literature, the literature of the ancient world, medieval literature, masterpieces of the Renaissance, and short fiction. In science, students can study animal behavior, ecological field studies, forensic science, marine biology, horticulture, astronomy, and geology. All the school's departments offer many AP courses and honors courses. At a time when art and music are being cut at nearly all public high schools, Meadowbrook offers scores of courses in the arts, music, and the performance arts. The offerings at Meadowbrook are more extensive than the offerings at many small colleges, including honors courses in art, music, band, and orchestra. Students can study theater by taking courses in acting but also in comedy and improvisation.

Students can choose from more than 100 clubs. These clubs cover a broad range of interests, including Big Brothers/ Big Sisters, the Economic Empowerment Club, Habitat for Humanity, Gender Equality, Peace Club, Model UN, Debate, and many, many more. Students at Meadowbrook are encouraged to think widely about the world and to sample opportunities to engage with the world and community in meaningful ways.

The combination of highly educated families and a school program that is enriched and expansive results in spectacular educational outcomes; the average SAT score in mathematics is above 700. That is the average. The mean score on the SAT verbal is over 550 and nearly 600 in writing. Only 6% of seniors taking the math SAT failed to score above 400. Meadowbrook students routinely win National Merit Scholarships.

The dominant culture is decidedly competitive; students are encouraged and cajoled to succeed academically, socially, and on the sports field. The key to educational success is a spotless academic and social record. This means getting good grades, "acing" the SAT exam (usually with the help of tutors), and success on the athletic field. Much of the educational project of Meadowbrook is organized around the careful calibration of what colleges want to see in successful applicants. Order rules: Punctuality, on-time home-work completion, competition for grades, test-taking skills, and outward respect for authority are the ground rules of the official culture. The teachers and administrators record and reinforce this paper chase through an elab-orate system of grading, testing, and monitoring. As future employees and leaders in large organizations, startups, and international businesses, the students grow accustomed to being watched, evaluated, and measured for competence.

Of course, much of what goes on in the classroom is an extension of the home. There is very little disruption between the home and school in upper-middle-class schools; family and school blend together in a seamless web not found in other class rites of passage. One of the subtle issues in the dynamics of class reproduction is that schools, generally, are not part of the lives of working-class and underclass families; they have little or no sense of ownership, and for many working-class and underclass parents, schools arouse painful memories and feelings of alienation. They lack a social pass-port for admittance. Because of work, many working-class and underclass families do not have the time to visit their children's school regularly. This is not the case in the upper-middle-class world. Because of their high level of educational attainment and high property taxes, upper-middle-class families have an active sense of taking charge of their children's education. School does not intimidate them; on the contrary, they happily criticize and work to "improve" the school by pulling political strings and marshaling parental support for their positions.

This close family and school connection is found in the classroom. Teachers and students talk about business regularly; it is a common teaching technique to ask students to imagine themselves as the head of a corporation, a role most students take on easily. In one social studies course, students were asked to write a business plan for an international startup as a class assignment. The world is a marketplace and the young CEOs in waiting are already preparing themselves for corporate leadership. There is not too much class or wealth guilt to be found in the classrooms of Meadowbrook, nor is there a great deal of concern about multiculturalism. Three percent of the students are African American.

The family culture is also expressed in students' dress and taste. Designer clothes are common, although the school prohibits revealing shorts and dresses. The dress code, however, is subtly sidestepped in a hundred little ways. Class culture is not something easily left outside the school door. When students in one class were assigned the task of creating an imaginary biosphere that would sustain human life in outer space, most did not forget to include personal trainers and yoga mats. Students evaluated each other's products on iPads. The student culture puts great stock in looks, a little swagger, and sex appeal—as do their parents. Students learn to party hard and most begin dating no later than their sophomore year. Meadowbrook students are quick learners, and by the time they are juniors they know how to play the game—a skill that will serve them well in the office, at the country club, and in their private lives.

The Definition of Self-Narrative

Mark is a Meadowbrook High junior well on his way to climbing the ladder of success. His father is the CFO of a transnational company, which means he is away from home a great deal. His mother is a stay-at-home mom, but serves on the boards of numerous local charitable and community organizations. She is an avid and excellent tennis player and travels to tournaments around the Northeast. Mark has a younger sister whom he seldom sees because she is constantly on the move with afterschool activities, parties, and academic coaching. The family communicates by cell phone, text, Facebook, and Twitter—Mark is never off his handheld device. His best friend at home is the family cook.

Mark is a good student, but weak in science. He frets that this deficiency will keep him out of Stanford, where his mother and father excelled. He also frets that his girlfriend is seeing someone else. In Mark's world, dating is a status game that is almost Darwinian in its competitive intensity. Although Mark is popular, he is far from being sought after by girls. He is attracted to the daughter of a local fireman in his class, but to ask her out would put him at risk of ridicule by his friends. Being part of a clique is an important survival strategy in socially competitive schools; dating a girl from the wrong side of the tracks might mean being snubbed by his buddies and their girlfriends. Mark is already trapped in the status game and is experiencing all the contradictions and conflicts that come with the need to be included in an exclusive social set.

Although private elite school students are explicitly told that they are the next generation of leaders, the leadership narrative at Meadowbrook is more implicit and lacks a moral imperative. The upper-middle-class rite of passage does not equate leadership with suffering or sacrifice. Materialistic America does not suffer from Calvinist guilt. Doing well and doing good are by no means mutually exclusive of each other. To put it another way, leadership in the upper-middle-class rite of passage is about material leadership. These are the children of the 1% and their worldview is generally not shaped by lofty and perhaps unattainable ideals, but by capital accumulation and the good life. If one can *do well and do good*, then so much the better, but doing well comes first.

Students at Meadowbrook have a positive image of themselves; success for them is not a distant ideal that will require sacrifice to attain. On the contrary, success is right around the corner and within their grasp. Their parents are role models, but so are the adults in the school. Like their upper-class peers, upper-middle-class students are empowered to see themselves as able to cope, perform, and be successful. The school, through its institutional practices, encourages in its students a positive self-image. As a group, students' self-esteem is apparent not only in their self-confidence but in their willingness to compete without reservation. They have control over their lives; their locus of control is firmly attached to an inner sense of efficacy and intellectual ability.

For minority students, attendance at Meadowbrook is both a blessing and a curse. On the one hand, they will graduate from one of the best high schools in the country, which will enable them to attend the most selective colleges and universities. The quality of their education will be high and they certainly will understand the world of the upper middle class. On the other hand, African American culture at Meadowbrook is nonexistent, except for the celebration of Martin Luther King Jr.'s birthday in January. The struggles associated with being non-White and poor in America are simply not part of the Meadowbrook rite of passage. Overt racism is not apparent to the observer, but a deeper kind of discrimination is obvious. People without resources are nearly invisible.

Whereas the girls at Highridge are earnest and modest in their dress, the young women of Meadowbrook are assertive and very sure of themselves. It is clear that they set the social agenda for the school and establish status hierarchies based on wealth, looks, and coolness. In class, they are far more likely to speak up than boys, and they establish the cultural tone for the school through complicated rituals of acceptance and rejection. Their class rite of passage prepares them for a life of intense sociability, status seeking, and organized fun. This is not to say that the girls at Meadowbrook are not interested in academic success; as a group they generally outperform the boys.

Because upper-middle-class high schools like Meadowbrook are a smooth extension of family values and ambitions, the school is able to solidify class values in the natural course of events. The student social life at Meadowbrook is intense. Pecking orders are established, cliques are formed, and the "cool" kids call the social shots. They see each other inside and outside of school at parties, sleepovers, trips, and family outings. They shop together, and yes, they drink and take drugs together. Families tend to form lasting friendships, and their children stay in touch in adulthood. Class consciousness is strong in the Meadowbrook community; shared taste is a distinction that identifies the upper middle class as a class apart and a class with social power.

Although the creation of collective memory may not be as intense, as frequent, or as emotionally powerful in upper-middle-class public schools as it is in elite boarding schools, it is still a very real experience for most graduates. Bonding lasts well beyond graduation; the upper-middle-class rite of passage is foundational for the business and professional class to consider itself a class-for-itself. This sense of solidarity is expressed in shared values and lifestyles. Most graduates of Meadowbrook will repeat the lifestyle of their families if they can afford it.

The role of the school in creating this sense of being a class-for-itself is decisive. It formalizes class values, fortifies them with the mantle of merit, and provides a channel to highly selective colleges and universities. It also provides a place where students can meet and collectively learn the values of their class. The school is the catalyst that turns the embers of class consciousness into intentional behavior and action. Collective memories become collective identities and shape the life trajectories of its graduates.

The upper-middle-class rite of passage prepares students to pursue professional careers leading to prosperity. These presumptive careers require education, discipline, and judgment. Although the upper middle class lacks the soft Calvinism of the upper class, it does place the future in the hands of real people in real time. Wishing on the stars is a good way to go bankrupt. The social order works for the upper middle class, and there is little incentive to challenge class relations. In fact, there is a marked disincentive to change the social order. The definition of self that most students develop may be liberal in terms of sexuality and social issues, but it is profoundly conservative in terms of social power relations. The definition of self-narrative for upper-middle-class students is the desire for a smooth highway to success and learning to play the game with ease. The upper-middle-class rite of passage is not meant to transform students as much as to confirm what they have already experienced at home and at school. The upper middle class, through its cultural and institutional power, is very much a class-for-itself, not through the adoption of an overt ideology, but through education and occupation. Competition is not something to fear; it is something to relish.

The Community Narrative

The community of the upper middle class is the comfortable home, the country club and the yacht club, the school, the selective college, and the company or professional office. Because we live in a globalized world and because much of globalization is in fact the internationalization of business, many Meadowbrook graduates can expect to lead lives of power and influence in the world. Their larger community is the network of corporate offices that ring the globe and control the flow of money. Life at the top is very different from life at the bottom or in the middle. For many members of the upper middle class, the globe is their playground. Private jets fly them to work and play, and when they arrive on distant shores, a limousine awaits.

CONCLUSION:
INSTITUTIONAL IMPACT AND COLLECTIVE MEMORY

Meadowbrook is a Mecca for those pursuing the American Dream of material success; like all religions, sacred and secular, it promises real and symbolic rewards for a life spent observing the rules. The American Dream, however, is not a religion without ambivalence and alienation; it tends to stifle dissident thinking and individuality. Students' life projects require consensus thinking, conformity, and allegiance to a collective class identity based on ownership and material display. Upper-middle-class public schools are in many ways hothouses where adolescents learn the lessons they need to climb the corporate and business ladder. But success can be a hard master.

Most upper-middle-class students internalize the master narrative of prosperity so deeply, it is more like breathing than thinking. It is close to an automatic social behavior. The cost of this rite of passage is difficult to detect from the outside because life is easy, fun, and optimistic. Yet, the economy of the psyche is designed so that becoming a member of any group, including a social class, requires giving up some part of the self to be accepted. The golden bracelet of extreme material success can be moral handcuffs that chafe against the skin of creativity and freedom. In reality, life for 99% of the world's population is not a party; it is a struggle. But if you are among the lucky 1% where the reward structure is unquestionably attractive and available, it is difficult to resist the temptation of withdrawing into the safe and comfortable world of the privatized marketplace self.

4

The Middle-Class Rite of Passage

THE FEAR OF FALLING

Riverside High is located in a suburb less than an hour's commute from New York City. The Riverside community is economically mixed; living alongside a few wealthy families are many middle-class and working-class families. Riverside is a community of less than 7,000 people. The town takes pride in its history and the role it played in the American Revolution; George Washington's army marched past the town on its way south to engage the British Army at Yorktown in Virginia. Old-fashioned civic pride and patriotism is expressed by numerous American flags flying in front of stores and homes and bumper stickers reminding us to support our troops. At the center of the town is a memorial honoring the many community men and women who died in service to their country. The town has a big Fourth of July celebration and in the warm months the parks are active with ball games and picnics.

The town supports four churches that are well attended on Sundays. Longtime residents dedicate newly planted trees in town to loved ones who have passed away. In many ways the Riverside community is a throwback to a bygone era when middle-class families were invested in their towns and each other. Small towns are becoming a thing of the past, but the families of the Riverside community are hanging on to old-time values with a sense of pride, but also anxiety. Because of the stagnant economy and the rate of inflation, there is a sense of slow decline and a "fear of falling" to use Barbara Ehrenreich's (1990) phrase to describe middle-class fears of descending the socio-economic ladder.

The architecture on Main Street is decidedly mixed, with old and new buildings standing side by side in different states of repair. Most buildings are in need of new paint and there is definitely a no-frills flavor. The majority of businesses have been operating for many years and outsiders are accepted only on a provisional basis—anything too edgy or unconventional is likely to find itself falling under the watchful eye of the town selectmen. The town supports several nail salons, pizza parlors, and dry cleaners. There is no bar scene and after 8:00 P.M. the town pretty much rolls up and goes to sleep. There are no chain stores in town; luxury foreign cars can be seen, but Chevys and Fords outnumber them. The local volunteer fire department is a major social center for many of the town's residents.

Most families in the Riverside community earn between $45,000 and $75,000 a year and there are a significant number of families earning between $10,000 and $40,000. The unemployment rate is 7% and due to the recent recession there is no job growth. Most residents work in middle management, small businesses, the teaching and human services professions, and retail sales. Eighty-two percent of the residents are classified as non-Hispanic White; 8% is of Asian background. The Riverside community is family-oriented; 40% of the households have children under the age of 18.

The town supports several low-income housing complexes and residences for its older citizens. The average house is estimated to be worth slightly less than $600,000, but this figure conceals a substantial amount of variation. A few Riverside community residents live in houses that have upper-middle-class amenities such as pools and expansive lawns; most everyone else lives in multifamily houses, apartments, and modest middle-class ranch-type houses. On a warm day the side streets off Main Street are filled with families sitting in lawn chairs, washing their cars, and cooking on the outside grill. The town elects a mayor and town council, and there is a lively local civic and political culture. There is a sense of order in town with a small and diligent police department.

The town's wealthier families often send their children to one of the two nearby private schools or to a boarding school. Most of the students who attend Riverside High come from middle-class and working-class homes. Several years ago, the town passed a bond measure and built a new middle school attached to the high school. The new complex includes a gym, a theater, and modern, if conventional, classrooms, science labs, and art studios.

Most students who graduate from Riverside High enroll in college, and a few attend socially selective colleges such as Georgetown, Duke, and Columbia. Most students, however, attend New York state and out-of-state public colleges and universities. The colleges in the New York state university system located upstate are particularly popular, as are large state universities such as the University of New Hampshire, the University of Delaware, and Indiana State University.

Riverside High is the school most Americans imagine when they think of a middle-class comprehensive high school. Although academically a cut or two above the high school attended by Archie and Veronica back in the heyday of public education, Riverside does not have the academic offerings or the outsized ambition of Meadowbrook High. Getting a good job and having a family are the core values.

The underlying metaphor for the middle class is community. Because families in the middle of the class system are being squeezed from above and below, there is considerable tension in middle-class families about how to remain middle-class in the face of an economy and society that is being globalized and increasingly managed by large corporations located in places far away from small-town America. In a society where upward mobility has been blocked and the real inflation rate is close to double digits, fears of downward mobility are well founded (Ehrenreich, 1990). Can Riverside High stop this slide downward?

THE MIDDLE-CLASS RITE OF PASSAGE

The middle-class rite of passage is about continuity, respectability, and community. Riverside High plays a very big role in the lives of middle-class families. The school is student-friendly with guidance counselors and enough athletics offerings so almost all students can be on a team. There is a feeling of constructive optimism about the school, and the leadership team is enthusiastic and connected to the community. The boundary between the community and Riverside is porous; many parents are involved in supporting the school. Riverside High is their social insurance policy against downward mobility. Unlike the students at Highridge and Meadowbrook, Riverside students do not arrive at the school door with a small army of tutors, coaches, and high-profile parents behind them.

Riverside enrolls a little more than 600 students; a typical graduating class is well under 200. Three percent of the students are eligible for free or reduced-price lunch. Eighty-five percent of the students are non-Hispanic White, 7% is Asian, with a small number of Hispanic and African American students. All classes are taught by what the state refers to as "highly qualified" teachers; there is very little teacher turnover. The school meets all state requirements for adequate yearly progress. Nearly all graduates receive a Regents Diploma indicating academic achievement and many receive an advanced designation demonstrating a high level of competence. The dropout rate is essentially zero.

The Architectural/Ascetic Narrative

Riverside High is located on a hill above town. As mentioned earlier, a new middle school wing has been attached to the old high school building built over 40 years ago. Unlike Highridge or Meadowbrook, Riverside does not have a great many playing fields. A football field is also used for all other outdoor sports, and there is a practice field up a dirt road, tucked away in the woods behind the school. Riverside has no lawns or rolling fields; the school backs up on a wood fence erected by a middle-class residential development. Parking is limited.

In many ways, the architecture echoes that of the small office buildings found in the local area. The style is functional, with no frills or details, no extras, no wasted money on charm, no individuality. But it is pleasant and inviting. Entering the school, the visitor is greeted at the door by a student or teacher and asked to sign in, no ID required. The level of trust is high; the visitor can walk around the school unaccompanied. There are some trophy cases with sports awards, but these are modest compared with Highridge and Meadowbrook. Riverside is a small school and does not compete in the top sports division. There are banners announcing upcoming events and there is a cheerfulness to the school that is inviting. Lining the halls are little handmade posters announcing the causes which students support and contribute time and money to.

The hallways are filled with student work and posters designed to promote hard work and fair play. Being fair and honest, along with service, is a recurrent theme. Recently, some students returned from Central America where they built houses for the rural poor, and there are pictures of their adventure on a large bulletin board. Classrooms are nondescript but roomy; teachers have decorated them according to their taste, which includes movie posters and posters of rock-and-roll legends—mostly from the era in which the teacher grew up. The school has several science labs and workspaces; the physical size and condition of the school is adequate, but by no means extravagant. There is, however, a very large art room where students can work on art projects and hang them in the halls. Unlike Meadowbrook, where students' art work is hung professionally, the student art work at Riverside is hung by the students themselves. This freedom of expression gives Riverside a feeling of youthfulness and even a little zaniness.

Most faculty members do not have offices and most help out with afterschool activities such as sports and clubs. Many faculty members began their careers in urban school settings and consider themselves fortunate to be teaching at a safe, academically productive middle-class school. The school's food service is standard fare but ample and relatively healthy. There is little conspicuous consumption; pizza and heroes are favored. There is little ostentation in the middle-class rite of passage. In fact, showing off is frowned upon. Unlike the school culture of Meadowbrook, where daring and even extravagance are favored, the school culture of Riverside is safe and predictable. The aristocratic airs of the upper class and upper middle class evaporate into thin air in the levelheaded atmosphere of Riverside.

The office staff at the school is composed primarily of women from the local community, who are friendly and keep the area outside the principal's office a beehive of sociability. Every student is known on a first-name basis;

Riverside is a home away from home—a community center as well as a school. There are group pictures of the faculty for each of the last 10 years on the wall outside the principal's office; team play is considered the norm, not the exception. Extreme individualism is not a Riverside value. It is easy to strike up a conversation with teachers and students who are pleasantly curious about the researcher's activities. Everyone is helpful, and when visiting classes the researcher was invited to participate. There is an equalitarian ethos in the school that is inclusive and unassuming.

Much of the school is enlivened with what can only be called touches of Americana, such as the painted mailboxes outside the college counselor's office that have upbeat messages about the importance of each individual. These positive messages are expressed by cartoon-like well-painted Disney characters and other happy woodland creatures. Pictures of the school's mascot are inescapable and newspaper clippings from the local papers about the school's successful athletic teams get pride of placement. Whereas the principal's office at Meadowbrook is spacious and corporate, the principal's office at Riverside is small and filled with school memorabilia, basketballs, posters, schools awards, and the principal's diplomas. There is a feeling of friendly and inviting chaos.

The Authority Narrative

The principal at Riverside began his career as a coach; he still is in excellent shape. He holds an advanced degree from a well-known school of education and is very active in the local school leaders association. He is a hands-on leader with a strong sense of service. He is seldom in his office, preferring to be in the hallways, classrooms, and at sports events. He performs in school plays and is an all-around champion for Riverside. Whereas the principal at Meadowbrook models a corporate leadership style, the principal at Riverside models a style of leadership attuned to public service and commitment to community.

The principal at Riverside is a cheerleader, a coach, and a father figure. School spirit, teamwork, service, and a general happy disposition are the values he personifies, setting the tone for the school climate. Because Riverside students do well on standardized tests, he has few problems from the state, and because he is experienced he is able to keep his school free from too much government interference. He does not have a grand or grandiose vision of his students becoming world leaders or corporate leaders—he is preparing community leaders.

He is the embodiment of the mid-level office manager whose most natural habitat is the small firm or local business. The school is small enough and family-oriented enough that he does not have to be too bureaucratic; he knows his teachers well and connects to them in informal friendship-based ways that encourage a sense of team play rather than top-down control. He is a team builder without a lot of noise about leadership. He runs a tight ship, but not one with the intense sense of urgency found at Meadowbrook. He is a near-perfect role model for students who are community-minded and intend to embark on white-collar careers.

For some of the newly arrived upper-middle-class parents the principal's leadership style is uninspiring. They are looking for a more aggressive and dynamic style of leadership. The middle-class rite of passage is not what they are looking for. In fact, they think the middle-class rite of passage is to be avoided at all costs; downward cultural and economic mobility is anathema to them. The current principal decided to retire in 2013.

The Pedagogic/Curriculum Narrative

Riverside offers a wide variety of courses, although not nearly as extensive as Meadowbrook. Graduation requirements are determined by state standards that include 4 years of English; 3 years of math, science, and social studies; and 2 years of foreign language. Essentially, the Riverside curriculum is a sturdy and predicable set of offerings. No frills, but the courses that are offered are solid. Students can take integrated algebra, global history, the living environment, and any number of biology, chemistry, and physics courses. French, German, Hebrew, Italian, Latin, and Spanish are available. The school offers 19 advanced placement classes. More than 200 classes are offered on a yearly basis.

Class sizes are small, hovering around 20 students per class. Classrooms are run democratically, and few teachers lecture. But order is expected. And so is on-time homework. When a student fails to do their work, teachers call home to talk with the parents. If a student misses three homework times, his or her grade is automatically dropped a whole grade. Practicality is important, and because the school is small, students are easily monitored and supervised. Riverside students do exceptionally well on standardized testing. On the state Regents exams, they scored at or above average more than 95% of the time. In U.S. history and government, 74% of those seniors taking the test scored above 85%. One hundred percent of the 37 students taking the Latin exam scored above 85%.

As mentioned earlier, Riverside's dropout rate is near zero. Ninety percent of graduates plan to attend a 4-year college after graduation. Much of this success goes to the school's leadership and teachers who put in long hours helping individual students and counseling students in need of extra attention. There is a teachers' union at the school, but there is little of the tension associated with unionization found in urban areas. Teachers put in long hours without necessarily referring to the provisions in their contract.

There are more than 50 teachers at Riverside. They have graduated from a variety of colleges and universities. The teaching ethos at Riverside is student-oriented; they know every student on a first-name basis. There are no slamming doors or loud arguments. In fact, there is a friendly give-and-take that signifies a high degree of trust.

Technology is used in the classroom, but Riverside is not jumping on the technology bandwagon. Soon the school will be wireless, but many websites are blocked because of their inappropriate content. Although the teachers use iPads and the Internet for teaching, there is still an old-fashioned loyalty to the book. In the parlance of today, Riverside remains a "high touch" school despite the widespread adoption of technology by many schools. Perhaps this is why Riverside students do so well; research and experience tells us that learning requires face-to-face interactions. Riverside is in many ways an extension of the families who send their children to the school. Hard work and honesty are prized. Learning is a practical necessity and moral duty. Team play matters, as does respect for others. Most students are not headed to top corporate jobs; they are headed to Middle America.

The Definition of Self-Narrative

Jessie is a senior at Riverside. Her mother and father graduated from Riverside, as did her older brother. Jessie is an average student and she has an afterschool part-time job at a pet grooming business in a nearby town. Jessie plans to go to college after graduation but her parents cannot afford the high tuitions of most colleges; she thinks that attending a nearby state college is the best possibility. Jessie likes the idea of helping people; her cousin, whom she admires, is a nurse. She would like to stay in Riverside and get a job. If she does not become a nurse, she might become a teacher.

She enjoys school and participates in a few afterschool activities, but generally, schoolwork does not really excite her. She likes most of her teachers but has no mentor or teacher who motivates her to stretch herself intellectually. She is friends with many of the staff as they live in town and she has grown up with them and their families. School is a pleasant routine where the unexpected almost never happens.

Jessie is a bit of a loner; she avoids unchaperoned parties and drinks sparingly, although many of her friends party every weekend. She doesn't have a car; her parents live in town and run a small dry-cleaning business. She uses her cell phone regularly, texting a small group of friends, and visits her Facebook page once or twice a week. Generally, she prefers to share a pizza with her family and boyfriend at home. If she were asked about her class awareness, Jessie would be baffled; in her worldview all good people are middle-class.

It is quite possible that in today's economy, where wealth is being transferred up, that Jessie's class may go the way of the horse and buggy. The future of the middle class is very much in doubt. The middle-class rite of passage, which at one time was the gateway to comfort and security, is being eroded. The cost of housing has pushed home ownership out of reach for most of the younger generation of the middle class; they are rapidly being supplanted by an aggressive, acquisitive upper middle class with more impressive educational credentials. The educational route of most middle-class students is not to the Promised Land of the American Dream but is increasingly headed to a place where opportunities are in short supply and actual poverty is quite possible.

There are few minority students attending Riverside. The few that do have a difficult time finding a safe social niche for themselves. The Riverside community is socially conservative and outsiders of all kinds are treated with some suspicion. People of color, in particular, are not welcomed with open arms. The local police are vigilant keeping young people from Yonkers or the Bronx out of town. This lack of acceptance means that students of color keep a low profile both in school and out of school. The psychic cost of this 21st-century invisibility for minority students is no doubt substantial. Their middle-class rite of passage is not likely to result in a strong sense of efficacy and an internal locus of control for them. They are outsiders with few attachments to the local middle-class society.

The middle-class rite of passage for girls can be characterized as having two contradictory tendencies. On the one hand, they are equal if not superior to boys academically, and there is no observable evidence that they are discriminated against in the classroom. The families that send their children to Riverside are not likely to shortchange their daughters when it comes to college and career. On the other hand, there are few role models for the girls at Riverside to inspire them to reach a little higher and expect more from life than marrying and raising another generation of Riverside students. Although girls are not disempowered, they are not particularly empowered, either.

Compared with the upper-class and the upper-middle-class rite of passage, the middle-class rite of passage is less likely to produce collective memories and collective identities. Today's middle class has lost much of its distinctive class identity and solidarity. Perhaps this is due to losing so much economic and political power in the last 30 years. There is a quality of drift in the middle class that is reflected in the culture of Riverside High. In contrast to student interactions at Highridge and Meadowbrook, the intensity, frequency, and emotional impact of the student interactions at Riverside are tame, sporadic, and lack a sense of group solidarity. Sporting events are often poorly attended, very few students volunteer for cheerleading, and school plays draw sparse audiences.

Riverside students are far less likely than Meadowbrook students to spend time out of school shopping together, playing together, and just hanging out, although some students meet in the woods to drink and socialize on Saturday nights. Many have afterschool jobs and many prefer to go home and study or pursue a hobby. There is little in the social life of the school that encourages lifelong loyalty. It would be surprising if many students felt any real emotional resonance or emotional connection to Riverside after graduation. Riverside is a good school but it is not a status maker that provides a deeply transformative experience for students. The middle-class rite of passage is weakly organized and lacks the vigor and drama of other rites of passage. The infusion process is not dramatic and lacks intentionality.

Collective memories are not as powerful in the middle class as in the classes above it because the ideology of individual achievement is strong and because the middle-class connection to the economy is as employees who are more likely to bond with their place of employment than with their class. Some of Riverside's graduates will remain members of the community, but being a community member is not the same as being a class-for-itself. Social action beyond the town to protect middle-class interests is not a part of the community's political agenda.

In some ways, the middle-class rite of passage disempowers all students because it prepares them for a future that most likely will not exist in coming years. This may well affect their sense of self-efficacy. The sense that the future belongs to someone else is expressed in the lack of ambition that many students exhibit. If a young man or woman cannot make things happen even though he or she has played the game, what internal dynamics take place? Most likely, ambiguity and self-doubt will grow with each passing year as the society and economy moves away from the middle class. The world of the middle class is changing very, very rapidly. The cultural capital so painstakingly accumulated by the middle class in the past has less and less market value. In today's world, the once robust and proud middle class has diminishing social power affecting its sense of being a class-for-itself.

The Community Narrative

For generations, the middle class has staked its social claim on educational amount, hard work, and respect for traditional values. The middle-class rite of passage is built on these assumptions. How will the middle class define itself in the new situation of blocked mobility? Will they double down on the American Dream or will they slide into increasing relative deprivation? Is the middle-class worldview sustainable in a wildly competitive marketplace world? And how will young people going through the middle-class rite of passage reconcile their beliefs with an economy that is increasingly a "winner take all" free-for-all, where the big prizes are won by the lucky, the upper class, and the upper middle class?

Historically, the American middle class has found employment, security, and respect in their local and regional communities. They were the white-collar workers who made the economy work for the most number of people. They were the backbone of the civic culture that made democratic politics possible. They held a commonsensical view of society and the world that was the moral ballast of a fast-growing and sometimes unruly society.

Today, local and regional communities are becoming the backwaters of an increasingly globalizing economy. The middle-class community is becoming more and more fragile and is in danger of disappearing. In this sense, the middle class has lost its public voice and has lost its community. For middle-class students undergoing the middle-class rite of passage, the future is unclear and the community they most likely would join may not be there for them when the time comes.

CONCLUSION:
INSTITUTIONAL IMPACT AND COLLECTIVE MEMORY

Surveys show that, generally, Americans think of themselves as middle-class; as a society, we have decided that *middle-classness* is akin to *classlessness*. American middle-classness is an aspiration for many of the poor and a place of anxiety for those who have already achieved it because life in the middle lane can be economically insecure. Historically, the institutional impact of middle-class schools on their students has been powerful because the ethos of middle-class schools was compatible with the ethos of the families who sent their children to these schools. But what happens when institutional impact pushes against a shifting social reality that is becoming less and less hospitable to the institution's message and purpose? What if the collective memories created at Riverside High are memories of a world that no longer exists?

If class memories have fewer and fewer real social references, they become more and more disembodied and more and more historical. The world that Riverside High is preparing its students for has many appealing and admirable features. In terms of class reproduction, however, we may be witnessing a significant shift in the American class structure. The basic five-class structure may be on its way to becoming a four-class structure: upper class, upper middle class, working class, and underclass. As we will see in the next chapter, even the American working class is under enormous strain and could, as a class, be in serious danger of losing social power.

5

The Working-Class
Rite of Passage

THE ROAD NOT TAKEN

Not far from Highridge Academy is Patrick Henry High School. The two schools are roughly the same size, but there the similarities end. The students at Highridge come from all over the world and are overwhelmingly members of the upper class, nearly all the students at Patrick Henry come from rural working-class families, struggling to make ends meet. It is a landscape of huge social contradictions. Both schools are located in a corner of America that has been historically agricultural, has no housing developments, and has no roadside billboards to blemish nature's beauty. Settled in the 17th century by Puritans pushing west from Boston and eastern New England, the area is composed of villages, once home base for farmers who eked out a living from the hard rocky soil. The American Revolution took root here; resistance to British rule was fierce and there are many monuments to those long forgotten battles.

Although the rest of the United States has experienced enormous changes in the last 200 years, this part of the country remains relatively unaltered—at least on the surface. It is the fantasy world of those clinging to a Norman Rockwell America. Tourists traveling through the area are awed by the pristine quality of the countryside, the clean air, and the rolling estates of the gentleman and gentlewoman farmers who bought the land from the original owners and have built grand second homes for themselves and their families in the manner of the old British upper class. It can look perfect, almost too good to be true. Most of us know, however, that perfection for one class almost always has a steep social price tag for another. Someone has to pay for another's elegant lifestyle. And so it is in the shared but separate worlds of Highridge Academy and Patrick Henry High.

There are essentially two classes in this pocket of America: the very wealthy whose money comes from investments, inheritances, and speculation, and the rural working class who have very little money, no investments to speak of, and, in many cases, no jobs. In the 1980s, this two-class system was reinforced and deepened when the first wave of the new rich discovered the area, bought up as much land as they could, and began what amounts to a modern-day enclosure movement; working farmers, whose families had cultivated the land for generations, had to sell their land and were forced to take odd jobs or be hired back by the wealthy as caretakers. Some of them were never employed again. Others did manage to find new employment in the areas of service, construction, transportation, sales, and hauling. Many of these families teeter between being working-class and being members of the working poor. Nearly all families will go through bouts of poverty, as does much of the working class nationally.

Traveling on the main well-paved roads of the area, it is easy to miss the dirt roads that lead into narrow valleys and up steep rocky hills where the working class, the working poor, and the impoverished live in small unpainted houses often surrounded by rusted-out automobiles and chicken coops. During the winter their houses are heated by coal stoves and fireplaces. Hunger is a reality and so is disease; many children do not see a doctor until they get inoculated for chicken pox, polio, and other childhood diseases before entering 1st grade. Some are luckier and are able to afford small ranch houses and serviceable cars, but they struggle for respectability—economic and social mobility is not part of the picture for these Americans. Today, the area is going through more difficult economic times than usual.

The unemployment rate is above 10% and many local residents have given up looking for work, or they work at odd jobs off the books. A few of the men travel long distances to find work in construction, hauling, and farming. The community has experienced negative job growth for many years, long before the recession of 2008. Most families earn between $15,000 and $70,000 a year; nearly 50% earn less than $50,000 annually. Forty percent of the town's residents rent their homes; the value of small homes has plummeted in the last decade. There is virtually no market for them. These people are the new working class, struggling to find a foothold in an economy that has moved most working-class jobs overseas. The town has seen better days; there are no chain stores, no supermarkets, no Starbucks; there is a gas station and a beauty parlor. This is one of the communities that affluent people rarely notice, driving through on their way to a vacation or an upscale destination. It is part of invisible America.

Every year at the town meeting, the school board presents the annual school budget. The wealthy landowners almost never attend these meetings. They are in New York or Boston and wouldn't attend even if they were in town. There is a sharp class divide that is almost never crossed. There is always a lively debate among the town folk about expenditures, with most of the town's residents resistant to raising taxes. In a small town everyone knows everyone else and everyone else's business, and people don't want to pay for someone else's business. People are still angry about the new patrol car the part-time police chief bought for himself several years back.

By far, the largest item to consider is the school budget, which is subject to close scrutiny. In an economically insecure world, it appears to many residents as though administrators and teachers have it cushy, complete with health coverage and retirement plans. There is a sense that the school is wasting money, even if the facts don't support these suspicions. There is an undercurrent of resentment against the school's staff who, compared with nearly all the town's residents, drive better cars, live in bigger houses, and go on vacations during the long cold winters.

Although a handful of middle-class graduates from Patrick Henry go on to well-known private colleges and universities such as Colby, George Washington University, and Emory, most college-bound working-class students attend state universities and colleges. Roughly 5% attend a state university such as the University of Massachusetts or the University of Vermont, another 25% attend a local state college, and 70% attend local community colleges within driving distance. The remaining students will look for work or enter the military.

In many ways, the working-class rite of passage is the road not taken. Few middle-class, upper-middle-class, and upper-class Americans understand the values, hopes, and fears of the working class. Yet, they rely on the working class to build their roads, grow much of their food, fix their plumbing, and fight the wars they start but expect the working class to finish. Except for TV sitcoms in which the working class is portrayed in buffoonish stereotypes, working-class life values and strengths are largely ignored by the media, academics, and intellectuals. Because working-class people have not had the opportunity to attend exclusive schools, they are often treated as backward, holding unfashionable cultural and political views. Today, the working class is all but forgotten by politicians (except at election time), policy wonks, and the media. It is our forgotten class; the working class built America, but today most working people have no place to live in the cultural mainstream and often do not own houses of their own in which to raise their families. They are the outsiders within.

THE WORKING-CLASS RITE OF PASSAGE

The underlying metaphor for the working class is class loyalty and patriotism. These are values that are felt with the heart and the head; they are not always fashionable, but they endure (Finn, 2012). The working-class culture of the students at Patrick Henry celebrates a rugged individualism and resistance to middle-class conformity. Many men in the community hunt and take pride in their collection of firearms. In the hills surrounding the town there are still pockets of self-sufficient communities. The worldview of these families is local and skeptical of outsiders. Administrators who fail to take this culture into account are likely to find themselves looking for another position sooner than expected.

The high school enrolls roughly 400 students with an even split between males and females; over 90% of the students at Patrick Henry are non-Hispanic White. Just over 20% of the students are eligible for a free or reduced-price lunch. The meals at Patrick Henry are basic: A typical lunch consists of chicken nuggets, juice, fruit, milk, and a salad bar. The menu is essentially the same every day except, for example, when chicken nuggets are replaced by hot dogs. For many students, this is their biggest meal of the day and it is common to see them loading their plates which extra portions of macaroni and cheese when it is available.

Government statistics concerning hunger in America downplay how many people are malnourished and underfed. There are millions of Americans who are not categorized as "hunger-challenged" but who nevertheless experience hunger on a regular basis (Cookson, 2011). Moreover, hungry people almost never receive the healthiest food. The cafeteria at Patrick Henry is small with a very meager selection; watching students crowd each other for an extra hot dog brings home this point powerfully.

The Architectural/Ascetic Narrative

Patrick Henry High is connected to a middle school in a one-story building complex that was renovated over 20 years ago. The school buildings are constructed of brick and cinder block with few architectural details. There is little landscaping and what there is consists of a few bushes and shrubs. Although the grounds are orderly and clean, the school has none of the graciousness and crispness of Highridge or the casual extravagance of Meadowbrook. Even though Patrick Henry is set in a rural environment, there are no large playing fields or any outdoor recreational facilities. There certainly is no ice hockey rink or golf course.

The fields that do exist are surrounded by tall pine trees that block the sun for much of the day. On the grounds is an old shed that was once used by principals when they needed to discipline boys who were truant or chronic cut-ups. As you enter the school there is a parking lot for teachers and the students who have cars to drive to school. Many of the students still take the school bus; owning a car of their own is only a dream. Most of the cars that students do have are on their last legs, with a noticeable lack of new paint and plenty of rust. Old pickups are popular; no BMWs or Mercedes. Because of budget cuts there is no late bus; if a student wants to be on an afterschool team or needs counseling or tutoring, he or she is out of luck. These students can't be on the team or get the counseling they need.

The school was built with cost savings and functionality in mind. The style echoes architecture associated with most state construction since the 1950s—no frills, few artistic details, and very little "wasted" space, although there is a large auditorium. Most public buildings constructed since World War II are not meant to impress those seeking architectural novelty and imagination, but to satisfy the demands of frugality and a public that wants nothing controversial or extravagant. The interior of the school is designed functionally: no large trophy cases, no paintings by famous artists, and no easy chairs. The floors are covered in linoleum and the walls are constructed of cinder blocks that have been painted a light institutional gray. The ceilings are low and covered with fireproof tiles. The hallways and classrooms are lit by industrial fluorescent lights. There are few windows, so the school feels dark and slightly claustrophobic. This sense of being closed in is accentuated because the school is not air-conditioned; there is little fresh air in the building. At the time of the renovation the school board thought it was too expensive to install and operate air conditioning; in the early fall and late spring the school has a sultry, hothouse atmosphere. State law requires that the outside doors be shut at all times and the windows can only be partially opened.

The hallways are dotted with bulletin boards posting school news, notifications, and some examples of student work. The network of halls is complex, much like unmarked roads veering off from multiple intersections. Student lockers line the halls; between class students have little time to socialize—they have 4 minutes to get to their next class, not too much time for chatting. Students at Patrick Henry are far more subdued than the high fliers at Meadowbrook or even the medium fliers at Riverside; life for Patrick Henry students is not a constant merry-go-round of parties and play. Nearly all of them have afterschool jobs or work for their families. They do not get allowances or a great many privileges. There are no afterschool tutors or private coaches. There are no family vacations to the Caribbean to think about. Life is very real and it is now. Patrick Henry students often dress in secondhand clothes—there is not a J Crew or Polo sweater or shirt in sight. The basic uniform is working-class: work boots, T-shirts, and jeans for the boys and plain blouses and jeans for girls. Shopping sprees are not a part of the working-class life; students here have few, if any, "crazy outfits." The preppy look of students at Highridge is from another world.

Life for many Patrick Henry students is hard, and often there is trouble at home. When families have few resources and few prospects, it is not uncommon for some members of the family to decline and become withdrawn, depressed, and hostile. Marriages are shaky and often break apart, bill collectors hound the family on the phone and sometimes in person, and relatives get in trouble with the law. So, when students gather to gossip, it may not be about who is going out with whom; it may be about who is getting out of rehab or having a court hearing. Young people have to grow up fast at Patrick Henry.

Between lockers are the classrooms, which are generally cramped and often decorated by the teachers according to their tastes. Many teachers have taken the opportunity to make their classroom a home away from home for the students, with things to look at, play with, and share. The teachers are aware that many students come from homes with few books or other cultural artifacts. Without this teacher-led effort to humanize the school, there would be little individuality at Patrick Henry. The school library is functional but by no means exciting. Increasingly, students are going online to find reference materials.

Discipline at the school is carefully defined. Skimpy dress is forbidden, as is gang-related attire. The student handbook emphasizes the authority of the teachers who "are in a position of authority in their classrooms and in all other parts of the school." The handbook also includes a section on "search and seizure," which formalizes the school's right to open lockers and search students if there is suspicion of "concealed firearms, drugs or other illegal materials." Students are warned that if they are in possession of any illegal substances or firearms, the police will be notified immediately. A student found guilty of selling drugs will receive a mandatory 2-year sentence and a fine up to $10,000. The basic philosophy of the school is tough love. But what is the educational message of these rules? Upper-class, upper-middle-class, and middle-class students would be hard-pressed to explain what mandatory sentencing means. The chances of a Highridge or Meadowbrook student being given jail time for selling a small amount of marijuana is virtually nil. At Patrick Henry the boundary between education and law enforcement is thin and easily crossed. Life is hard and students need to get tough to survive.

The Authority Narrative

The principal of Patrick Henry graduated from a public college with a bachelor's degree in physical education and a master's degree in exercise physiology and outdoor education. He is a no-nonsense school leader. His office is simple. The school staff is composed of women who live in the community and graduated from Patrick Henry several years back. There is a sense of family among the staff. They are not corporate; they are the backbone of the community, taking care of the community's children. It is still the case, however, that in working-class communities men are generally in positions of authority. There is a clear hierarchy at the school; the principal is in charge in the same spirit that the football coach is in charge of a team. He has the best interests of the team at heart and is not overly fond of slackers or the self-indulgent. He is friendly, confident, and does not appear to have an ounce of social pretension. He doesn't imagine he is educating the next generation of world leaders.

The head of Highridge and the principal of Patrick Henry may have similar jobs and work within a short drive of one another, but from a class culture perspective, they live and work in separate universes. The former is educating self-styled world leaders; the latter is educating those who will, with few exceptions, work for those world leaders as caretakers, carpenters, and maids.

It is not uncommon for working-class high schools to hire coaches as principals for three reasons: Coaches work well with students, coaches are natural disciplinarians, and coaches fit well into working-class cultures. The school committee overseeing Patrick Henry is composed of local citizens who generally are suspicious of the intellectual airs and social pretensions of the overeducated, impractical, intellectual class who graduate from elite colleges and universities. Although it would be nice to have a principal who had an educational vision, it is far more important that he or she run a tight ship.

To be a coach of a local team in working-class America is a position of status, and it is not by chance that many of the coaches at Patrick Henry are alums of the school. They are community members who are loyal to the cultural values of working-class America and enjoy the physical challenges and camaraderie of competition. Sports are not only an outlet for the working-class love of physical activity; they represent working-class values: team play, loyalty, and grit. As role models for young adults, the coaches exemplify old-fashioned paternalistic authority: They are firm, fair, and not very tolerant of deviance or difference. Nonetheless, Patrick Henry teams often struggle on the field against local high school teams; the talent pool is not deep and many students do not participate in school sports because they have to work after school. The authority narrative at Patrick Henry is similar to the authority narrative of the military—if you follow orders, all will be well; step out of line, however, and punishment will be swift and none too subtle.

Firmness is a signature quality among administrators. Although most students at Patrick Henry are willing to follow rules, there is a substantial minority that resists authority. Working-class students are apt to come from homes where there is little attention paid to developing academic creativity. Flights of fancy are likely to be seen as silly or worse, indicative of an unbalanced mind. When this rejection of intellectual and creative pursuits is combined with family instability, resistance to school is quite possible. The principal must be a good counselor; he may well be the difference between stability and breakdown for students who have nowhere else to turn for adult support. He is able to connect to the working-class culture, which admires resistance and independence, while at the same time showing compassion and having a clear understanding of the risks that many working-class adolescents face. If they mess up and fall from grace, there will be no safety net to catch them.

Students at Patrick Henry have not been deeply socialized into traditional academic middle-class values. In fact, in many cases they openly resist middle-class convention. Low-level conflict is common; the principal's unofficial job is managing this conflict with a firm hand. From a class reproduction perspective, the leadership style of the school is highly compatible with the authority structure found in most working-class places of employment. There is a clear chain of command, and success on the job requires acceptance of top-down authority.

The Pedagogic/Curriculum Narrative

The curriculum of the school is basic and aligned with the state curriculum frameworks. Unlike the elaborate mission statements of the more affluent schools, the mission statement is straightforward. Students are expected to communicate effectively, develop critical thinking skills, and be able to use information resources and technology. In order to graduate, students must earn 24 credits. Of those, four are in English, three in social studies, three in mathematics, three in science, one in wellness, and two electives. The remaining credits may be earned outside of school through an approved extension program, an approved distance learning program, or in summer school. The curriculum at Patrick Henry is a model of the standard American high school curriculum; there is a set course of study with few frills. In English, for example, students are offered Standard English I, II, III, and IV. If they qualify, they may take Honors English I, II, III, and IV. Two AP courses are offered, as are four electives. Compared with the English offerings at Highridge Academy, the English offerings at Patrick Henry are adequate but hardly inspiring. School is school. This sense of a generic curriculum can be found in other subjects. The mathematics department offers 15 courses, ranging from Algebra I to honors calculus, with no frills and no AP courses. The music department offers five courses that include chorus. The social studies department offers 15 courses, including one AP course; ten of those courses are on American history or American civics.

This focus on American history is telling. In a globalizing world, students at Patrick Henry do not have many opportunities to explore other cultures and develop a cosmopolitan worldview. The idea that high school students should, at taxpayers' expense, study what many local people consider impractical subjects about foreign cultures runs counter to community beliefs about the value of education. Too much education can drive out common sense.

The school does have a technology department, offering courses such as digital multimedia production, video production, 3-D design, robotics, and a virtual high school option that is operated by a for-profit company. The school also has a vocational department with courses in food preparation, cooking, culinary arts, clothing, early childhood education, construction, carpentry, and woodworking. Afterschool programs include arts enhancement, Future Farmers of America, garden projects, the school newspaper, yearbook, and Students Against Drunk Driving.

The curriculum is broadened by partnerships and internships with local organizations. The carpentry class, for instance, built a goat barn on campus with Future Farmers of America and a town storage shed in partnership with the police department. Students studying economics can intern at a local plastics factory and those studying science can intern at a local fish hatchery. The school has a partnership with a local community college where students can take AP courses and enroll in a dual-credit high school-college program. There is little grade inflation at Patrick Henry; the cumulative GPA is approximately C-plus. The combined average math and verbal SAT score is just over 1,000. Twenty percent of students take an AP course by the time they graduate. Thirty-five percent of the students are enrolled in remedial courses in math, English, and writing.

There are 35 teachers at Patrick Henry, some of whom also teach at the middle school. The teaching staff is evenly divided between males and females and most have taught at the school since the year 2000. With less than a handful of exceptions, the overwhelming majority of teachers received their bachelor's degrees from small public institutions, including state colleges in New England that were previously normal schools preparing teachers. Some of the younger teachers are pursuing master's degrees and a small number of faculty members in the arts and vocational departments do not have degrees, but have obtained state specialty certifications.

If a family has no history of college attendance, there is a strong like-lihood that their children will be less likely to enroll in college after grad-uation than the children of college graduates. In a recent graduating class, there was only one student who was the first in her family to enroll full-time in college, which was a local state university. Eleven first-in-family students attending college enrolled in a local community college. Eighty percent who enroll in a community college return for a second year. On average, students earn a C-plus their first year in college.

The pedagogic/curriculum narrative of Patrick Henry is conventional and intellectually comfortable. It also includes a significant vocational com-ponent. The development of a free-floating questioning life of the mind or acquiring knowledge for knowledge's sake is not part of the learning cul-ture. From the perspective of linguistic code theory, the students at Patrick Henry are exposed to a restricted code. Imaginative flourishes are not en-couraged; Patrick Henry students are not encouraged to see themselves as the makers of a larger, more cosmopolitan culture. In truth, their culture lives at the margins of the mainstream. The world Patrick Henry is prepar-ing its students for is rapidly becoming history.

The Definition of Self-Narrative

There is a toughness of spirit in working-class families that is often missing in the upper and middle classes. Take Tom, for example. Tom grew up in a two-family house a block away from the school. His father attended Patrick Henry, although he did not graduate. His mother graduated from a Catholic high school in a neighboring town and worked as a payroll clerk in a local plastics extrusion plant until it shut down due to Chinese competition. His father is part owner of a local bar and moonlights as an unlicensed plumber when he can find work. Tom's brother is in the Marine Corps; Tom plans to join the Marines after graduation. Tom has a cell phone; he uses it to con-tact his buddies and keep up with sports scores. He has yet to sign up for Facebook; he and his friends are more apt to shoot baskets than spend hours social networking. Tom has a girlfriend, but they are not close; he doesn't really "get girls" and secretly fears his girlfriend will become pregnant if they go "too far." Honor would require them to marry.

Tom is a good football player but is a little undersized for college ball; he dreams of going to the local state university when he gets out of the Marines, but he will have to balance work with school. One reason he is joining the military is to get a small scholarship that is offered after dis-charge. For Tom and his friends, school is about jobs; his view of society is starkly realistic. His class rite of passage is a no-frills journey—loyalty to family and friends, patriotism, and personal pride are the things that matter. He knows about the rich, stuck-up people from New York and Boston who own the big second homes and estates, but in his worldview they might as well live on the moon.

Patrick Henry students do not go on fabulous vacations to Europe, nor are they given a car for graduation; they rarely visit a big city and when they do they can't wait to get home; they seldom know anyone who has achieved professional status. The only contact they have with rich people is mowing their lawns and plowing snow from their long driveways for ten dollars an hour. They have driven by Highridge and watched the prep school students stroll from building to building dressed in the mysterious garb of the prep upper class. Do they envy those lucky children? Of course they do. Sadly, envy can easily turn to self-hatred.

Working-class students are seldom pampered or told they are special. Just the opposite—toughness and independence are the prized values that matter in the real world. For many working-class students, high school is an imposition to be endured and escaped. The rite of passage for the students at Patrick Henry and other working-class schools is, in Paul Willis's words, "learning to labor" (1977).

Patrick Henry sends a powerful message to its students—success in the world of work means not asking too many questions, accepting authority, and not questioning the current social order. Students' social horizons are set relatively low and their frames of reference are usually narrow, centering on what *is* rather than what *might be*. This is not to say that all students happily fall into line. On the contrary, there is resistance to the school's program of soft authoritarianism and plain vanilla education. Working-class students are not passive. They resist by shutting down, by talking back, by taking drugs and drinking, and by creating a student culture where intellectual excellence is seen as acting snooty. In some ways, the school is fighting an uphill battle because the world is changing so rapidly that, to some students, the old-time values the school stands for seem to come from a different planet.

In the end, however, the majority of students accept the hands they are dealt because their role models are solidly conventional and alternative lifestyles are not part of the picture. Learning to labor leaves little room for self-exploration and departing from accepted ways of thinking and living. From a class reproduction perspective, working-class students learn to be working-class adults because to depart from traditional values would be very difficult. There are times when holding on to working-class values can feel more like ankle bracelets than wings (see the work of Jean Anyon, 1980, 1981, 2006, for a sensitive portrayal of the life of working-class students).

Patrick Henry has virtually no minority students. The few that do attend lead separate lives. Not far from the school is the town where the great early-20th-century African American intellect and leader W. E. B. DuBois grew up. In his autobiography DuBois writes about discovering discrimination in the foothills of New England. Not too much has changed in the last 100 years.

Working-class gender relations are also something of a throwback from a middle-class perspective. The girls and boys at Patrick Henry do not mingle as much as the students at Highridge, Meadowbrook, and Riverside do. In many ways, they live in different cultures. For the girls at Patrick Henry, life is hard. They are expected to help at home, bring in extra money, not cause trouble, and marry early. Going away to college is not part of the family or community equation, although a few try to break free every year. The school does little to encourage the girls to test themselves academically on the assumption that they will remain in the community and continue the lifestyle of their parents. Many will become pregnant in high school or just after graduation.

How strong are the collective memories and identities of Patrick Henry graduates? Are they on the way to becoming members of a class-for-itself? Historically, the American working class has at times acted as a class-for-itself and at other times a class-in-itself. Working-class radicalism was either repressed or co-opted in the era of industrialization. The rural working class has had periods of populism and radicalism, but these periods have been episodic rather than continuous. Compared with European working classes, the American working class has porous boundaries, little ideology, and often aspires to become middle-class.

Students at Patrick Henry do share many powerful collective memories, but most have been generated by growing up working-class; the school acts as a reinforcer rather than a creator. The school's contribution to the working-class rite of passage is important, as it brings students together and subjects them to a "treatment," but because the school has so few resources its capacity to hold students' attention is minimal. This, however, does not mean that Patrick Henry students do not undergo a socially formative rite of passage or do not share collective identities.

Being working-class is a very strong identity. It is bone deep. The class infusion process begins on the day of birth and remains in place for a lifetime. Primary values such as loyalty to family and country are everyday values that are not instilled by reading or intellectual struggle. The role of Patrick Henry in reinforcing these values is not to challenge them, but to elevate them as the core values of school and of life.

Social life at Patrick Henry is not intense: Dances are sparsely attended, sporting events draw few student spectators, and for many students school is the place you don't want to be. Nearly everyone has an afterschool job and many are one of their family's breadwinners. There is no time or money for shopping, chatting, or hanging out. The leisure time allocated to upper- and upper-middle-class children does not exist in a world where the specter of hunger is real and ever-present.

We see the paradox of the American working class being acted out in the culture of Patrick Henry. The working class does have a distinctive rite of passage and working-class high schools play an important role in rein- forcing the class infusion process, but the working-class rite of passage is removed from much of the larger society and remains somewhat self-rev- erential and outside the mainstream. Students at Patrick Henry are deeply socialized into their class culture as a class-for-itself, but it is not entirely clear what they are being socialized for in the context of other class rites of passage. If the end game is not power, prosperity, and security, what alterna- tives are available to working-class youth in 21st-century America?

Working-class adolescents are in some ways irrepressible. Liberated from middle-class status anxieties and repression, they are free to feel, fight, and develop a robust sense of humor. To be working-class is not a punish- ment; it can be an invitation to live life with gusto and guts. Patrick Henry is a laboratory for studying adolescents who are largely unfettered by the paper chase or self-conscious selfless service. It is a place where students get into trouble, laugh, and, occasionally, demonstrate academic brilliance in spite of the odds.

The working-class rite of passage teaches students to accept external authority as legitimate and to look outside themselves to find their locus of control. Power is externalized and individualism is minimized. There are few elements in the working-class rite of passage that would help most students gain a strong sense of self-efficacy and feel able to cope, perform, and be successful in the larger world. In place of middle-class white-collar aspira- tions, the working-class rite of passage emphasizes nonintellectual—though laudable—values of loyalty to class and patriotism. In part, working-class solidarity results from opposition to the dominant class of "bosses" and intellectual elites, but that is not the whole story. Working-class families believe in mutual support and family.

Unfortunately, the working-class rite of passage can be disempowering from the perspective of upward mobility and agency. The American work- ing class has developed an alternative culture in which many middle- and upper-class values are disowned but, in the process of rejecting mainstream values, much of the working class is left disempowered. The soft authoritar- ianism found at schools like Patrick Henry fosters an externalized locus of control. Unquestioned loyalty to class and flag means giving up significant parts of the self to forces that are above and more powerful than the indi- vidual. There is a reason why so many of America's armed forces are staffed by working-class men and women at the enlisted level; they accept authority and have been socialized to accept the social order as good and worth dying for. Willingness to die for a cause in which an individual has no immediate stake requires an external locus of control that is deeply embedded in working-class culture.

The Community Narrative

Nearly all the graduates of Patrick Henry will enter blue-collar or minor white-collar trades and services. They will either not graduate from college or they will graduate from a local state or community college. They are very likely to marry early someone they have known in high school or who comes from the same town or surrounding area. Most will live in or very near the locale where they were raised and, in general, repeat the lifestyles of their families.

In a rapidly globalizing world, this local perspective can be a handicap. Many of the graduates of Patrick Henry have little awareness of the larger world, the forces that are shaping the future, and the opportunities that are available to them. If the world were stable and change were slow, such a worldview might not be exciting, but it would not be dangerous. But the world of work is being systematically shipped overseas by American corporations and the small business and industrial infrastructure that supported much of the American working class is disappearing. Many of the graduates of Highridge Academy will become leaders in the corporate and political worlds, and I am skeptical about whether they will consider the needs of Patrick Henry graduates when they make decisions that affect the manufacturing and financial markets. The economic future for many of the graduates of Patrick Henry is not bright (Weis, 1990). If they remain in the local area, there is a very good chance they will go through extended periods of unemployment. In a period of decline, the working class falls at a faster rate than the middle class because their economic base is much more fragile.

CONCLUSION:
INSTITUTIONAL IMPACT AND COLLECTIVE MEMORY

What do students at Patrick Henry High really think about class in America? It is wrong to think that working-class students have little or no understanding of the class structure—they are often very shrewd observers. Looking at class power from the outside gives them a grasp of reality that is often missing from the worldview of the privileged. Rites of passage are not linear; they are dialectical. Working-class students assess quickly the difference between what they are told to be true and what they know to be true; nobody is going to take care of them—they have to take care of themselves.

The class infusion process in working-class schools is systematic and charters working-class adolescents to become working-class adults. The confluence of messages leaves little room for developing alternative narratives, and most acts of resistance are overcome by the school either directly through discipline or indirectly by inculcating the norms of compliance so deeply that only the bravest or most daring can break free. Working-class solidarity may not be manifested with the same self-conscious confidence and verbal skill as the classes above it, but it is similar in intensity and pervasiveness. Unfortunately, many of the collective memories of working-class students are social blinders that shut out social peripheral vision and condemn many young adults to a life of labor without much hope of upward mobility.

6

The Underclass Rite of Passage

THE SEARCH FOR DIGNITY

Roosevelt High is located in the South Bronx. According to the 2010 census, the 16th Congressional District, which includes the South Bronx, is the poorest in the United States—43% have incomes below the poverty line. According to the Institute for Children, Poverty & Homelessness (July 2011), 47% of the people living in the South Bronx worry about being homeless (p. 1). The Bronx itself is a microcosm of America; 28% of its residents live below the poverty line, yet one of the country's most affluent neighborhoods, Riverdale, is just a quick ride from the South Bronx. The Bronx is 42 square miles with a population of 1.4 million; nearly double the size of the population of Montana. It is the third most densely populated county in the United States.

The Bronx has a storied history; waves of Irish, Italian, Polish, and Jewish immigrants found their way to the Bronx in the 19th and 20th centuries. In 1937, 44% of the borough's population was Jewish, but in the 1960s and 1970s European immigrants left, often moving to lower Westchester County or Florida. The most recent immigrants are from Puerto Rico and the Dominican Republic. Fifty-four percent of the Bronx's population is Hispanic and 30% is non-Hispanic African American. It is the home of hip-hop, the biggest metropolitan zoo in the United States, and the New York Yankees.

The Bronx is the most northern of the five boroughs of New York City and is the most diverse in terms of class, race, and ethnicity. It has been calculated that there is a 90% chance that any two residents chosen at random will be of different ethnicities or come from different countries. Thirty-three percent of the residents are foreign-born; 44% of the population under the age of 5 does not speak English at home. Thirty percent of the residents are under 18 years old.

Population density produces its own kind of magic and misery. On the one hand, the human story is played out every day in all its variability, intensity, and confusion. It is a sociologist's paradise. People are not stuffy; humor and irony make the lack of privacy just bearable. It is all out there for everyone to see—there is no hiding behind white picket fences or in exclusive clubs. You need to be real to survive in the craziness of a madcap, swirling world of endless movement, noise, and street life. The bridges, highways, and railroads of the Bronx are the most heavily traveled in the United States. The borough never sleeps, and people learn to watch their backs. The streets of the Bronx are not for the soft or sentimental; hip-hop was not invented by a church choir in the Midwest. The Bronx is in your face.

The streets bordering Roosevelt High are lined with bodegas, Laundromats, pawn shops, fix-it shops, beauty parlors, and fast-food restaurants. There is a busy street life around the school where people gather to talk, eat, and play music. For many, the street is home because their small and overcrowded apartments are cramped and uncomfortable—steaming hot in the summer, icy cold in the winter.

Roosevelt is a small high school that was founded during the chancellorship of Joel Klein. Located in one of the most famous school buildings in the Bronx and the city, Roosevelt is one of four small schools housed in the building. Just over 400 students attend Roosevelt: Seventy-two percent are Hispanic, 26% are non-Hispanic African American, 20% are ELL students or English language learners, and 20% are special education students. Just under 50% are female; every student is eligible for the free lunch program.

The New York City Department of Education has developed a "College Preparatory Course Index." According to the index, to be college-ready, a student must pass one Advanced Placement exam or its equivalent. The city average is 30%; Roosevelt's average is less than 10%. Another measure the city has developed is "The College Readiness Index," which measures the percentage of students in a school who pass a Regents exam and/or pass out of remedial coursework at the City University of New York. By this measure, less than 6% of Roosevelt's students are ready for college. Recall that all the students at Riverside passed the Regents exam and we have a simple measure of what educational inequality means in the lives of poor young people.

THE UNDERCLASS RITE OF PASSAGE

The underlying metaphor for the underclass is the search for dignity. Being poor is not just another thing in a child's life—it is everything (MacLeod, 1987). Life is crowded, hard, and sometimes violent. Childhood development in the traditional middle-class sense is a luxury. It takes courage and grit to survive and keep hope alive. Poverty is a street school that teaches students that life can be short and often brutal and you have only yourself for protection. Violence is expected, and it is not unusual for young people in areas of concentrated poverty to be treated as apprentice criminals. The police department has a policy of "stop and search," which it exercises regularly in the South Bronx, but seldom on Madison Avenue in Manhattan. When students pass through Roosevelt's airport-type security system, they must empty their pockets, open their backpacks and if they set off a metal detector alarm they are subjected to a body search. The building has a contingent of uniformed security guards, and if there is trouble or suspicion of trouble, New York City police officers are called in to walk the halls and question students—in public, in the halls. Teachers monitor the halls regularly and restrooms are locked during class periods. Clearly, the educational environment at Roosevelt is dramatically different from that of the schools I have previously described. Statistics tell only part of the story. A visit to Roosevelt tells the human story.

The Architectural/Ascetic Narrative

The South Bronx is a historic community and many of the buildings in the neighborhood surrounding Roosevelt High were once the homes of upwardly mobile immigrant families. Today, almost all those buildings are in need of repair. Roosevelt itself is a relic from a bygone era. Originally designed as a large comprehensive high school, it retains some feeling of the late Victorian period, with its wide halls, high ceilings, little decorative details, and an auditorium complete with stained-glass windows. It is easy to imagine how it appeared in its heyday when the city took pride in its neighborhoods and invested in public education.

Today, the building is a maze of poorly lit halls, staircases, and classrooms that feel cramped and uncomfortable. It is hard to fit 21st-century education into a 19th-century building even though the staff tries diligently to work with what they have. In many ways, Roosevelt mimics the buildings the students call home. Life is chaotic and there seems little incentive to spend much time investing in maintenance. To be fair, there is some repair work being done—slowly, very slowly. The school has no fields, playgrounds, or outside recreation facilities. A high chain link fence surrounds the staff and teacher parking lot. The school is surrounded by a main thoroughfare and residential streets. Fresh paint is in short supply, and in general there is a sense that tables, boxes, and chairs are left to sit wherever they happened to land. The administrative offices are cramped, with no amenities, and the teachers' lounge is part lounge, part storage room, and part workroom. The level of cleanliness in the school leaves something to be desired; the furniture is old and in need of repair.

There is some student work on display in the hallways and individual teachers make an attempt to decorate their classrooms with student work and materials that they have either bought themselves or were provided by publishers. Often, these displays reveal how resource-poor the school is and how many students at Roosevelt struggle with the basics in writing and organization. The student work is sprinkled with uncorrected misspelled words and poorly constructed sentences and paragraphs. There are sheets of paper about school—"*dos-and-don'ts*"—tacked to the walls, along with a few posters of famous Americans, complete with their most repeated inspirational quote. No one is looking at these rules or quotes. Nearly all the essays are about life in the Bronx and the students' hopes to find a better life. The students at Roosevelt have hope despite the odds.

Getting around the school is a challenge; signage is in short supply and the visitor must rely on the kindness of strangers to get directions. Unlike the other four schools in this study, Roosevelt feels disorganized and chaotic. Dark stairwells designated as "downstairs" are used for going upstairs, and the opposite is also true. In general, the lighting is dim and the old wood floors creak underfoot. Students are wandering around the halls between classes and during class periods; the back of the school is a parking lot. The noise level is intense—shouting and door slamming is common. There is an edginess to the atmosphere that partakes of the streets outside.

Students do not have money to buy new clothes. Style is important to teenagers; the style at Roosevelt is *street,* including oversized sports caps for boys and short shirts for girls. Unlike wealthier children, the students at Roosevelt are not loaded down with technological devices and the latest gadgets; most have discount cell phones, which they hold in their hands as they walk and talk.

Many of the students are hungry. As mentioned above, 100% are eligible for the free lunch program. But what does that really mean in human terms? More than a million American kids go hungry every day; ten blocks from the White House, 35,000 children go hungry every day. It is fair to say that all the students at Roosevelt have experienced hunger, some episodically, some chronically. Meals provided by the school are basic—there are no frills. Most of the food is unhealthy but filling. The search for food is part of the school culture—who has it and will they share? I was asked by the administration what I was bringing for the students as a way of thanking them for talking with me. I have never been asked this question before. At first I was baffled, but the principal, seeing my confusion, made a suggestion: "Bring food—they like food, they like pizza." I brought pizza with me on the days I visited. There is no surplus of anything at Roosevelt, including the basic services students need in an environment of scarcity.

Roosevelt isn't just old, funky, and in need of repair and a thorough cleaning; it has some of the characteristics of a poorly run prison. As mentioned earlier, students must pass through a security checkpoint when entering the school, entrances and exits are closely guarded, and the students are monitored on a minute-by-minute basis. Like many schools in areas of concentrated poverty, Roosevelt is, in reality, a soft prison. This doesn't mean that the teachers and administrators choose to run the school in a constant state of quasi-lockdown. They know more than most the cost of treating students like criminals-in-the-making, but their degrees of freedom are limited. The New York City Department of Education imposes security regulations in the name of staff and student security. The reality, however, is that students end up being treated more like inmates than students.

The Authority Narrative

Urban schools attract some of the nation's most dedicated and hardworking principals. Leading and managing a school in a neighborhood where the unemployment rate is above 40% and over 20 languages and dialects are spoken requires a full quiver of leadership skills. Moreover, most urban schools are seriously underresourced in relation to the needs of the students and the faculty. The greatest challenge, however, is not the students or the parents; it is the politics of the city and the endless paperwork required by New York's Department of Education. The reporting systems that have been put in place at the city, state, and federal levels in the name of accountability strangle creativity. The paper chase requirements of governments, far away from the life of schools, are forcing urban school leaders to become masters at gaming the system.

The leadership of the school is hardworking and dedicated but nearly buried beneath this mountain of paperwork. Much is written about principals being instructional leaders and innovators, but the reality is that in schools located in areas of concentrated poverty, principals are asked to do a great deal more than organize curriculum and supervise teachers; they must be police officers, community connectors, and clever bureaucrats. The hardworking principal of Roosevelt cares about the students and staff and has established a positive relationship with the community. But it's an uphill battle. He wears many hats: community liaison, instructional leader, disciplinarian, city employee, and building manager. His office is really a closet with a small window and his staff is minimal. He gets out of his office regularly and knows the students by first name. In other words, he is dedicated to the mission of the school no matter how huge the obstacles.

From the perspective of class reproduction, however, the leadership style of the vast majority of urban principals is that of an overworked and underappreciated civil servant. The leadership model he or she presents is not thought leader, CEO, or coach; it is the embattled advocate who is most likely to lose most of the battles that matter. The authority narrative at Roosevelt is a daily story of hoping that no major crisis develops and that the role of leadership is very local, very fragile, and very contingent on events. Making change is difficult; the bottom line is that leadership is an exercise in pleasing the powers-that-be downtown at the mayor's office. What lessons do students draw from this model of leadership? They learn that authority is top-down *and* ineffective. Student input on decision making is zero. It is no wonder some students resist so strongly the fragile authority of the school—they have no stake in what happens—a theme that is played out on the street and in the neighborhood.

The Pedagogic/Curriculum Narrative

One of the most startling things that greets a visitor to most schools located in areas of concentrated poverty is the skimpiness of the curriculum offerings. Most textbooks are out of date and teachers use workbooks regularly. iPads are nonexistent, as are laptops. There is little cohesion to the curriculum map of most schools, including Roosevelt. In fact, I suspect that most administrators and teachers would be hard-pressed to explain the rationale behind the school's curriculum. Many lessons are created at the spur of the moment and the use of technology is sporadic and random: Uploading a lesson or game without framing it in a logical and sequential learning progression borders on entertainment. Many students are disengaged or asleep. Many are chatting with their friends and some are withdrawn and hostile. The learning environments are boring at best, adverse at the worst.

Teachers vary in terms of their knowledge of subject areas and pedagogical skills. Some are admirably courageous, giving 100% to their work, but others appear to be walking through the day. My conversations with them tended to focus on their obstacles rather than hope. Most are exhausted from the tensions and conflicts that characterize their working conditions. They receive little support. Although those who have tenure are happy to have job security, they too feel that the current reform regime is leaving their kids behind. They have almost no resources to work with, and at the end of the day, the only measure the city is interested in is test scores, making drill-and-kill the favored pedagogic technique. You get what you measure and, by any measure, the greatest educational output of the current testing regime is boredom. The testing regime so beloved by educational standardizers kills any spontaneity or genuine questioning in schools for the poor. We have dumbed down the learning experiences of poor students to the point that it is little wonder so many drop out before graduation.

It is not uncommon for students to act out, talk while the teacher is talking, and forget their homework. Yet, many students are hungry for knowledge; they have hope for a better future. Teachers often employ novel teaching techniques to keep the attention of their students, such as singing

and making references to popular culture. Schools that educate the poor are noisy, with lots of shouting, opening and closing of doors, and loud conversation. Loud bells regulate the school day. Some classrooms have a Smartboard, and teachers use them to varying degrees of success. Most of the teachers are young and are still learning their craft; a great deal is expected of them in a difficult teaching and learning environment. As in most schools located in areas of concentrated poverty, many students come to school conflicted by family turmoil. Most of them lack basic medical attention; if their eyesight is poor, they may or may not have glasses. It is hard to see a Smartboard lesson from the back of a classroom if you can't read what is being written.

The school uses a portfolio approach to student work, but must still cover the traditional subjects mandated by the state. In order to graduate with a Regents Diploma, students must earn 44 credits in academic subjects: eight in English, eight in social studies, six in science, six in mathematics, two in visual arts, two in second language, five in health and physical education, and seven in electives. In order to pass a Regents exam students must score 65 or better. To be awarded a "local" diploma, students still need 44 credits and score of 55 or better on the Regents exam. The school offers two AP courses in English and Spanish. New York City also has instituted a number of citywide tests in certain subjects, including Earth Science, English, Geometry, Global History and Geography, Integrated Algebra, Living Environment, and U.S. History and Government. With the exception of U.S. History and Government, the scores Roosevelt students earn on these exams are well below the scores of other students attending public school in New York.

The school offers some afterschool programs, including limited sports, a student newspaper, theater, internships, a junior reserve officers training corps, robotics, a Japanese club, and a Spanish club. The school has a partnership with a local community college, and most of the graduates who do go on to college attend units of the City University that are essentially open admissions, although a few students attend New York state colleges. Almost none of Roosevelt's graduates attend private colleges or universities. Many will enter the workforce, some will join the military, and others will return to the street.

Roosevelt is one of hundreds of high schools operated by the New York City Department of Education. Much of what happens at the school is in response to the department's mandates. The department has put in place a number of management tools by which to evaluate Roosevelt's AYP (adequate yearly progress). Roosevelt's overall academic and administrative grade is B. In terms of student progress in meeting the state's academic requirements Roosevelt earned a B in 2011, an A in student performance as measured by the percent of students graduating (65%), and a C in school environment as measured by student attendance, safety, and engagement. The department's scoring metric ranges from "underdeveloped" to "developing," to "proficient," to "well developed." Overall, Roosevelt is rated "proficient." The single item in which Roosevelt received a "well developed" in academic year 2010–2011 was for creating a culture of mutual trust and positive attitudes toward learning. The school is struggling to improve its rating.

Notwithstanding the school's poor performance, the parents who send their children to Roosevelt give the school high marks. According to a Department of Education survey, 96% of Roosevelt's parents were satisfied or very satisfied with the education their child received at Roosevelt in 2010–2011. Seventy-two percent of parents feel that order and discipline are maintained at the school. Overall, Roosevelt's rating is comparable to the ratings of other high schools in the city—Roosevelt's scores on academic expectations, communications, engagement and safety, and respect hover around a seven on a one-to-ten scale.

The class infusion process is powerful in underclass schools, and if curriculum is a relay for power relations, then the curriculum of Roosevelt and other similar schools relays powerlessness. There is little attempt to develop the individual geniuses of the students or to push them intellectually. A general anti-intellectualism pervades the school; there are virtually no opportunities for students to study in depth or explore nonbasic topics. The academic rite of passage for poor students is a narrow, rocky road, an intellectual journey to nowhere.

The Definition of Self-Narrative

Shawna is a senior at Roosevelt High and grew up in the South Bronx. She shares an apartment in the neighborhood with her mother, two sisters, brother, grandmother, and her mother's boyfriend. Shawna works part-time at a local Laundromat folding clothes and keeping an eye on the machines. She wants nothing more than to escape the South Bronx; she dreams of being a singer, a doctor, a teacher—anything that will lift her out of poverty and allow her to live with respect. She has an inexpensive cell phone and keeps in touch with her friends continuously, almost obsessively. She does not have a boyfriend and, in general, has a deep suspicion of men.

Shawna works hard in school; her mother wants her daughter to escape the South Bronx and believes that education is the best and only route to a better life. Shawna particularly likes social studies and reads everything she can find about African American history. She admires African American women writers and secretly thinks she could be a writer. Unfortunately, the average class size at Roosevelt hovers near 40; many of her teachers barely know her name. Shawna keeps her dreams to herself; she hopes to be admitted to City College, but has only average grades. She is nervous about taking the SAT exam because she knows it might shatter her dreams of escape.

Because virtually all the students at Roosevelt are of color, the urban underclass rite of passage is racially inclusive, but in a way that reinforces racial and ethnic isolation. Most of the students have little social contact with White middle-class students; the only White non-Hispanics they meet are most of their teachers. The new segregation that has occurred in American education since the 1970s means that few poor students of color encounter students from a different class or a different culture—and vice versa.

Girls at Roosevelt face many obstacles to success. The boys tend to dominate the school physically and speak to girls in demeaning, often highly sexualized terms. If girls are not aggressive in speaking up in class, they are likely to be silenced or subjected to ridicule if it is apparent that they are intellectually competent. Female teachers often try to protect the girls, but street life dominates the halls of Roosevelt, making the job difficult, if not impossible. In general, schools like Roosevelt are rough-and-tumble places where young women are at risk. Most develop a hard shell in order to survive and protect themselves from dangers that are real.

Compared with the other class rites of passage discussed so far, the underclass rite of passage is a rough journey filled with collective memories that remind students that their chances of success are limited. The collective identities that are created at Roosevelt are a continuation of the street identities that residents of the Bronx must adopt to survive in a very tough world. Being tough and street-smart are virtues, and hiding your feelings under demonstrations of bravado provides a shaky sense of self that might otherwise dissolve in the hot water of desperation.

The social life of the school is largely unplanned; the general sense of chaos that pervades the school can be found in the social life of students. Down one of the halls hang the class pictures of students from days past. These students are well dressed, clear-eyed, and look eager to conquer the world. This is not the world of Roosevelt high today. Today's underclass rite of passage reinforces failure.

What self-image can a child develop having been exposed to the underclass rite of passage? What does the internalization of powerlessness do to a child's sense of efficacy? Poor children, unless they are very lucky, are exposed to a school system that teaches them they are powerless. The intense underclass class infusion process instills in most students a sense that they live at the margins of the American Dream. With some exceptions, they have difficulty imagining a life of success outside the Bronx because viable alternatives are not part of the school culture.

The underclass rite of passage is about the search for an elusive dignity. In terms of adolescent development, many students at Roosevelt lack basic trust and a positive self-image. There is little in the underclass rite of passage that would make students feel like they can cope, perform, or be successful. In the face of these obstacles, students' resilience, bravery, and hope are startling. Returning to the observations of Bandura (1993), "The stronger the perceived self-efficacy, the higher goal challenges people set for themselves and the firmer is their commitment to them" (p. 118). Poor people have very little control over their lives. Living day to day, worrying about life's basic necessities, fearing violence, and witnessing suffering and early death is not a formula for feeling empowered and having a strong internalized locus of control.

From what we have seen so far in this study, it is a reasonable hypothesis that the higher the social class background of a school's student body, the greater the likelihood that its class rite of passage will include feelings of efficacy and self-confidence. Collective memories are formed by the interactions of the personalities in the school. The institutionally forged collective memories of the students at Roosevelt narrate the ups and downs of continuous struggle and the ever-present reality of possible failure.

The Community Narrative

Most students who attend Roosevelt are very likely to stay in the neighborhood; life on the street is likely to be the moral and physical geography that these young people will inhabit. The community narrative for poor children is about survival and marginal employment, with long periods of unemployment. The underclass class infusion process prepares students for this life by internalizing powerlessness and a foreshortened view of the possible. Poor students do not expect to be world leaders. In fact, if they should express such desires they would most likely be mocked. What they do care about is dignity. Feelings of worthlessness are unbearable. The struggle for dignity is often expressed as having "face." Face is important in poor communities because it is the street equivalent of self-worth.

CONCLUSION:
INSTITUTIONAL IMPACT AND COLLECTIVE MEMORY

The underclass class rite of passage creates class consciousness as surely as the other class rites of passage do. Students at Roosevelt undergo a class reproduction process that is all-encompassing. They are surrounded by messages of powerlessness. The five organizational narratives reinforce the master narrative that poverty is, in reality, inescapable for the overwhelming number of students. It might be comforting to deny the power of the infusion experience at Roosevelt, but that would be unreal.

The collective memories of underclass young adults are powerful. They share a social and economic experience that is white-hot with emotion, frustration, and struggle. Their identities are forged in opposition to the dominant culture. These oppositional identities seem at times to be self-destructive, but in the context of the life these students lead, opposition is the last and best way to hold on to a sense of worth and pride. Although their understanding of society may lack the polish of a prep school or an upper-middle-class student, underclass students have a firm grasp of the basic facts of American life today. They know that power is real and that the social order is a hard reality.

7

Bending History Toward Justice

*The world changes according to the way people see
it, and if you alter, even by a millimeter, the way
people look at reality, you have changed the world.*
—*James Baldwin*

When Horace Mann called public education "The Great Equalizer" in 1848, he hoped it would interrupt the process of social reproduction and provide all students with equal opportunities to develop their talents (Cremin, 1957). If Mann were to return today, what would he think? I suspect he would be bored to tears by our endless arguments about educational policy. Mann was first and foremost an educator. Because he cared for children, he would be appalled by the physical condition of many schools and the boring curricula so many children have to endure. He would shutter at the sight of children bent over their desks filling in bubbles on standardized tests. But most of all he would be outraged by an educational system that prevents mobility and favors the already favored. His Great Equalizer has become the Great Unequalizer.

Mann shared the same democratic dream that animated the country's founders (Cookson, 2011; Cremin,1957; Ravitch, 2010). Thomas Jefferson and James Madison, in particular, understood that a universal, free, and educationally effective system of public schools is the foundation of democracy. In an 1810 letter to John Tyler, Jefferson wrote (Cookson, 2011),

> I have in mind two great measures at heart, without which no republic can maintain itself in strength: 1. That of general education, to enable every man to judge for himself what will secure or endanger his freedom. 2. To divide every county into hundreds, of such size that all children of each will be within reach of central school in it. (p. 18)

Madison was even more explicit about the importance of equality of educational opportunity for democracy's survival. In his 1810 State of the Union Address, he was impassioned about education's possibilities calling for a national "seminary of learning" (Cookson, 2011):

Such an institution, though local in its legal character, would be universal in its beneficial effects. By enlightening the opinions, by expanding the patriotism, and by assimilating the principles, the sentiments, and the manners of those who might resort to this temple of science, to be redistributed in due time through every part of the community, sources of jealousy and prejudice would be diminished, the features of national character would be multiplied, and greater the extent given to social harmony. (p. 18)

If Jefferson and Madison were to return today, what would they think? Would they trust we had lived up to their ideal? I think they would be deeply disturbed, realizing that we have created a school system that allocates quality education according to class and sorts and selects children according to the wealth of their parents (Oakes & Rogers, 2006).

In this last chapter, the major findings of this study are summarized: We consider their social and educational implications, and I propose a framework for breaking out of our current moral and intellectual dilemma, concluding with the question asked by George Counts nearly a century ago: Dare the school build a new social order? I ask this question with a sense of urgency; time is running out for the Great Equalizer. As I write, public education is being dismembered by the private sector and conservative politicians; we may be on the verge of losing public education altogether. This appropriation of civil society is compounding the major social and economic crises confronting us. Ostensibly, we are a democracy, but increasingly we are taking on the economic and social characteristics of an oligarchy.

Political scientist Jeffery Winters (2011) convincingly argues that democracy and oligarchy are not opposites. He underscores that democracy has won major victories in recent decades including, "spreading civil rights, improving the status of women and the ending of unpopular wars" (p. 18). On the other hand, democracy has proven powerless when it attempts to limit the financial reach of the wealthy. Winters notes the huge differences in the material power of the wealthiest 400 Americans and all the rest of us. To defend their fortunes the wealthiest have created the "income defense industry." According to Winters, "The essence of oligarchy within democracy rests on the near-veto power oligarchs retain on threats to concentrated wealth" (p. 22). The consequence of this revolution from above is that the public sector has been impoverished. The top 1% has reframed the narrative of democracy into a narrative of entitled privilege. Class privilege is becoming more entrenched, not less. How distant this view of democracy is from that of Thomas Jefferson and James Madison! The monopolization of assets can take many forms, educational credentials among them. I believe real reform will not come from above; it will come from below (Cookson,

2011). And as I will propose, real reform must take the form of a massive overhaul of our education system. But first, what have we learned about the power of class reproduction?

THE SOCIAL CLASS DIVIDE IS WITHIN

We began this journey into the unspoken and generally unacknowledged social purpose of education by asking: How does the class-based organization of schooling structure the formation of social classes and what are the institutional practices of high schools that forge class consciousness in students? Although much is written about educational reproduction, there are few studies that look inside the "black box" of schools and examine how high schools reproduce educational and social inequality with such consistency and predictability. Answering these questions requires a new and different way of looking at high schools. I set out my approach in a series of propositions:

1. High schools are stratified by the social class backgrounds of the students who attend them. I hypothesized that there are two primary mechanisms by which high school students are sorted and selected by class: credentialism and the internalization of collective memory. Collective memory bonds classes internally and separates them from other classes. Collective memories are the substance of shared consciousness. This internalized class consciousness shapes worldviews and is connected to where a person goes to school and with whom, which in turn determines individuals' life chances.
2. The development of collective memory is possible because the institutional life of schools is based on intense emotional interactions and relationships, which deeply affect adolescents' emerging identities. Using the analogy of schools as theaters, I argued that schools create collective identities. I argued further that collective identities are forged when students undergo distinctive class rites of passage. Rites of passage are effective socializing mediums because they are repetitive and lead to the permanent internalization of collective memory.
3. I suggested that this internalization process is best thought of as an infusion experience that is embracing and enduring, creating collective memories of class solidarity.
4. The primary research strategy utilized to uncover how high schools construct their respective class rites of passage was comparative. By

contrasting the institutional values, practices, and class assumptions of five representative high schools arrayed across the five major classes in the United States today, differing class rites of passage were systematically observed and compared.

I suggested that my argument would be confirmed if the analysis revealed distinct differences in school-based rites of passage and that these rites of passage were correlated to class position. If the weight of the evidence and the clarity of the logic was convincing, we would have a *prima facia* case confirming the study's central hypothesis. We have just finished examining five class rites of passage in five high schools; how successful was this endeavor in uncovering how inequality is reproduced from the inside out, and what have we learned about what needs to be done to transform the Great Unequalizer into the Great Equalizer?

From the evidence we have examined, I believe there is a compelling case to be made that the social design of American high schools reproduces classes through the formation of collective class memory. Although the creation of class consciousness is not the only factor determining students' educational and life chances, it is a significant contributor to the inequality of opportunity. High schools are organized to infuse students with a strong sense of their class position; the infusion process is the foundation of stratified class consciousness. Schools are complex theaters of transference where the real lessons of life are taught through a deep curriculum that includes architecture and ascetics, authority relationships, pedagogy and curriculum, lasting lessons about students' social identities, and telegraphing to students their most likely adult communities of destination. The infusion process is an experience that stamps most students with the values and beliefs of their class.

Social class rites of passage charter high school graduates to take their allocated places in the class system. This is not accomplished by conspiracy or overt coercion, but rather through the day-to-day operations of schools, the cultivation of deep curriculum, and what appears to be common sense. Class reproductive processes need not be perfect to be effective; they are a broad and deep form of socialization that does not rely on single events or individual people. Class formation is structural and systematic, but that does mean it is not flexible or adaptive. Not every student needs to be successfully infused with class consciousness for classes to reproduce themselves. But most students are predictably and consistently infused with the beliefs, prejudices, and fears of their class because the processes of class infusion are powerful. It is a comprehensive form of socialization, which operates at conscious and unconscious levels.

High schools create inequality through class-based sorting and selection mechanisms and also by subjectively transforming the psyches of adolescents into instruments of class continuity.

High schools are well designed for creating collective memories. Infusion is not a mystical process; it is based on shared experience, emotional intensity, and the need to belong to a status group. Students go through their rites of passage together; they learn to share the same public voice, the same view of what is important in life, and the norms of behavior that are appropriate for *people like them*. Collective memory fills us with images of people and places upon which to anchor our class identities. Schools seldom interrupt the formation of class identity.

The journey from being a class-in-itself to a class-for-itself is not a walk in the park or a ramble down a country lane; it is a well-traveled road with clear directions, few detours, and almost no alternative routes. By the end of this process, our social class has been deeply internalized; it is within. The consistent and predicable reproduction of inequality is no mystery. It is baked into the system.

This finding is problematic for those of us who want a more equal and just society. It is hard to challenge the status quo and social order if inequality is baked into the system and the consciousness of students. But humans are inventive, adaptive, and creative. We need not be stuck in the trap of class conformity. Breaking out of the moral dead end of socially induced inequality is difficult, but worth the effort. In fact, it is the hinge of history, and we try mightily to bend history toward justice. Inequality is not like the weather—it is made by humans and it can be unmade by humans.

REFRAMING AND RESTRUCTURING

Sociologists have spilled much ink on the subject of the social order because it is a fundamental fact of social life. They have put forth functional, conflict, and evolutionary arguments about society's tendency to continuously return to what might be thought of as its default social structure. As I suggested earlier, social structure is slow to change. But it does change. If we see the potential for change, we might not be paralyzed; the point of social analysis is to develop a right course of action, which results in a desired outcome. To my way of thinking, the problem of the social order needs to be reframed into a challenge of social change.

Our high schools are relics from the past in terms of their capacity to bring about meaningful change. They are feverishly reproducing an industrial society that is inching toward extinction. The industrial model of education was designed for a world of work that required conformity and class consciousness. Today, we are developing an economy based on knowledge, service, and innovation. We are experiencing the greatest knowledge exposition in human history, but our school system is stuck in a repetitive cycle of re-creating an outdated social wheel.

We need a transformative ideal that is forward-looking, dynamic, inclusive, and seizes the creative possibilities within our grasp. While collecting data for this book I was talking with a Roosevelt High teacher when he mentioned that the mayor had recently given a speech at the school about how his policies were improving public education in the city. The teacher had a slightly ironic smile.

> It was kind of funny. A few days before the mayor gave his speech, they painted the front of the school but left the rest unpainted. I guess impressions matter in politics—too bad they didn't finish the job for the kids.

History has a way of repeating itself. As legend has it, Grigory Potemkin, a minister of Catherine the Great, created whole villages of fake façades to impress the queen when she visited the war-torn Crimea in 1787. The expression *Potemkin Village* entered into our vocabulary to signify an impressive façade to hide an undesirable fact. Many of today's educational reforms are Potemkin Villages. They look real but actually there is very little behind the façades except smoke and mirrors. Without honestly coming to terms with the stratification of schools, we will continue to deceive ourselves that rhetoric can trump reality. Unless we make deep and real structural changes, our educational system will continue to reproduce inequality with unerring predictability.

WHAT WILL IT TAKE?

To begin the task of creating a just and imaginative system of schools we need to think differently. In the last 2 decades we have fallen into the policy trap of thinking that a thousand micro-improvements will somehow result in real, significant, lasting change. This is an illusion; structure, especially class structure, will trump cosmetic reform every time. The microencapsulation of social problems is the counterpart to the conservative policies of social containment. Heroism has its place in mobilizing people to take action, but without an analysis based on data and a politically astute strategy, heroism tends to be solipsistic and self-reverential.

To break out of our reform rut, we need to reframe the debate. Cognitive scientist George Lakoff (2004) describes reframing as follows:

> Frames are mental structures that shape the way we see the world. As a result, they shape the goals we seek, the plans we make, the way we act, and what counts as a good or bad outcome of our actions. In politics our frames shape our social policies and the institutions we form to carry out policies. To change our frames is to change all of this. Reframing is social change. You can't see or hear frames. They are part of what cognitive scientists call the "cognitive unconscious"—structures in our brains that we cannot consciously access, but know by their consequences: the way we reason and what counts as common sense. (p. xv)

How could the education reform debate be reframed? What does re-structuring mean in practical terms? In previous work I suggested that we start with a firm and irrevocable commitment to the educational rights of all children (Cookson, 2011). This position implies that we need to make structural changes in our school system. We need to reframe the debate from focusing on individuals and personalities and instead focus on restructuring a broken system. Reframing can help us stop thinking of schools as isolated buildings with no real connections to the communities they serve (Bella et al., 1987; Kalhenberg, 2001; Kania & Kramer, 2011).

Given the current spirit of the times, this might seem like a utopian project. But history is a force that keeps on rolling even if we cannot see it move day to day. There are many signs of a new consciousness developing in the United States and throughout the globe (Iscol & Cookson, 2011). Nobel Prize–winning writer Toni Morrison, at a 2011 graduation speech at Rutgers University, beautifully expressed the personal importance of pur-suing something bigger and more lasting than ourselves: "Personal success devoid of meaningfulness, free of a steady commitment to social justice, that's more than a barren life; it is a trivial one. It's looking good instead of doing good." There are many men and women today who are rolling up their sleeves and making the world better one step at a time (Iscol & Cookson, 2011).

But individual effort and good intentions are not enough. Spirit with-out an understanding of the importance of human solidarity and collective action is unlikely to bend history in the direction of basic fairness and equal opportunity. We need to restructure. But where would we find an example of how education can be restructured for excellence and justice? As it turns out, there is an unlikely example of how modern school systems can be turned right side up.

THE FINNISH POSSIBILITY

When I first heard the buzz about how educational reform in Finland might be a model for educational reframing and restructuring in the United States, I was skeptical. Finland has a population of 5.5 million; the United States has a population of more than 300 million, composed of many competing ethnic groups. There are more than 1.3 million public school students in New York City alone, speaking over 100 languages and dialectics. The histories of Finland and the United States are dramatically different, as are the two country's economies.

But as I began to explore the issue I saw that although the countries are very different, the underlying challenges they face are similar. As Finnish educational reformer and author Pasi Sahlberg (2011) writes:

> The demand for better quality teaching and learning, and more equitable and efficient education is universal. Indeed, educational systems are facing a twin challenge: How to change schools so that students may learn new types of knowledge and skills required in an unpredictably changing world, and how to make that new learning possible for all young people regardless of their socioeconomic conditions. (p. 1)

My initial impression of Finland was that its class structure is essentially flat and therefore comparisons between the United States and Finland on the issue of class mobility were likely to be an analytic dead end. But upon digging further, I discovered that Finland is a country where class counts (Organization for Economic Co-Operation and Development [OECD], 2010; Riihela et al., 2002). Although income and wealth inequality in Finland is nowhere equal that of the United States, a recent OECD (2010) report found that the worldwide recession hit Finland harder than most other OECD countries. The report found that "Although income inequality remains low by OECD standards, it has increased substantially in recent years in spite of decreasing unemployment until recently. The incomes of the high earners have increased disproportionally since the early 1990s."

An earlier study (Riihela et al., 2002) found that total inequality rose significantly during the latter part of the 1990s. So, although Finland may not have the huge social contrasts created by concentrated poverty and concentrated wealth found in the United States, it is a society that is struggling with the disparities in opportunities caused by income and wealth inequalities.

Beginning in the 1980s, educators and the public in Finland came to terms with the fact that without overhauling their public education system they were going to be shut out of the global marketplace and Finland would continue to be a country where the birth lottery determines life chances. Educational reformer Andy Hargreaves, in the foreword to Sahlberg's book *Finnish Lessons* (2011) describes the principles of the Finnish reform:

Finland . . .
- Has developed and owned its own vision of educational and social change connected to inclusiveness and creativity, rather than renting a standardized vision that has been developed elsewhere;
- Relies on high-quality, well-trained teachers, with strong academic qualifications and master's degrees, who are drawn to the profession by its compelling societal mission and its conditions of autonomy and support—compared with the rapid entry strategies of short-term training and high teacher turnover advanced in countries like England and the United States;
- Has an inclusive special education strategy where nearly half of the country's students will have received some special education support at some time before completing 9-year basic school, rather than the special education strategy of legal identification, placement, and labeling of individuals favored by Anglo-American nations;
- Has developed teachers' capacity to be collectively responsible for developing curriculum and diagnostic assessments together rather than delivering prescribed curricula and preparing for the standardized tests designed by central governments; and
- Has linked educational reform to the creative development of economic competitiveness and also the development of social cohesion, inclusiveness, and shared community within the wider society. (pp. xix–xx)

All these policies are well within the structure of American public education. Jefferson and Madison easily could embrace the Finnish vision because, in Sahlberg's words (2010), "The Finnish experience shows that consistent focus on equity and cooperation—not choice and competition—can lead to an education system where all children learn well" (p. 9). He continues, "Education in Finland is seen as a public good and therefore has a strong nation-building function" (p. 39). Finland is a mirror to us; after all, we were among the first of the modern nations to link education with building civil society and a strong nation. Equity and cooperation are etched into the American political soul; universal, free, high-quality public education is the foundation of our society.

Although the Finnish experience shows that meaningful change can happen when there is enough political will, it would be naïve to think that we can import the Finnish basic school into America and expect it to be well received. We are a restless, contentious people accustomed to getting our way, suspicious of government. In our minds, we are rugged individualists. To begin the long journey to justice we need to embrace a wholly different approach to the creation of public policy.

A 21ST-CENTURY THEORY OF CHANGE

Imagine graduating young men and women from high school with open in-quiring minds, moral courage, and an eagerness to serve the common good; imagine young men and women who are self-confident and full of energy and wholesome pride; imagine walking into a school where genuine learn-ing is going on; imagine a school where every child, no matter what his or her family background might be, is given the opportunity to develop his or her talents; imagine a school connected to the world through technology and curricula; imagine a school where instead of mass education, we have personalized and customized education; imagine a school where every child feels cared for and protected; imagine a school that welcomes parents no matter what their backgrounds (Cookson, 2011).

This ideal is not pie-in-the-sky—it is within our grasp. Real change, however, requires a compelling metaphor. My favorite metaphor for thinking of change is the structure of oceans. Oceans have five "zones": the sunlight zone, the twilight zone, the midnight zone, the abyss, and the trenches. The lower one goes, the colder the water and the less movement. Most educational reform floats along the surface of the shallow sunlight zone, causing waves but never changing the game. Waves are not perma-nent, and after they wash up on the shore they retreat back to the sea. To change our class-based school system we need to restructure at a deep level; we need to get into the trenches. We need to dive deep and get to the cause of our dysfunction.

This requires a theory of action that is more than a sound bite. Shuffling the deck chairs is a pointless exercise when the ship is sinking and the passengers most likely to drown are not those in first class but those in steerage. We need a wholly new redesigned ship to carry us through the rough waters ahead.

In writing *Sacred Trust: A Children's Education Bill of Rights* (2011), I was inspired by the vision of the founders and Franklin Roosevelt. In his famous 1932 address to the San Francisco Commonwealth Club, Roosevelt talked about the need to have faith in ourselves as a people:

> Faith in America, faith in our traditions of personal responsibility, faith in our institutions, faith in ourselves, faith on our demands that we recognize the

new terms of the old social contract. . . . [F]ailure is not an American habit; in strength of great hope we must all shoulder our common load. (quoted in Cookson, 2011, p. 10)

Educational policy needs a social and ethical framework if it is to be coherent and grounded in long-lasting civic values and faith in ourselves. I am convinced that every American child and young person has:

1. the right to a neighborhood public school of choice that is funded for excellence;
2. the right to physical and emotional health and safety;
3. the right to have his or her heritage, background, and religious differences honored, incorporated into study, and celebrated in the culture of the school;
4. the right to develop individual learning styles and strategies to the greatest extent possible;
5. the right to an excellent and dedicated teacher;
6. the right to a school leader with vision and educational expertise;
7. the right to a curriculum based on relevance, depth, and flexibility;
8. the right of access to the most powerful educational technologies;
9. the right to fair, relevant, and learner-based evaluations; and
10. the right to complete high school.

To accomplish these goals, we need to rebuild our school system from the ground up; we need a community-based, grassroots theory of action that empowers and enables people to become the authors of their own destinies. We need to lift the dead hand of inequality off our collective shoulders and be free to develop fresh ideas that are inclusive, productive, and life-affirming.

But what would such a policy process look like? Today, we are so mesmerized by credentialism and top-down leadership that we have forgotten that in democracy real leadership and change begins with the citizens. An effective grassroots approach to policymaking could emerge along the following principles:

1. Begin with the people who live with the problems.
2. Listen to what the community needs.
3. Include all the stakeholders.
4. Find low-cost, local solutions that can be managed by local people.
5. Use the power of common interest to create a culture of constant improvement.
6. Link communities together in a constructive national conversation.

7. Ensure that our national values of democratic participation
   guide domestic and foreign policy.
8. Regain our respect for government as an ally in the struggle
   for justice.

These principles are commonsensical. If we are to transform the Great
Unequalizer into the Great Equalizer, we need a change of heart and mind.
We might begin by thinking of schools as embedded in communities and
start the hard but needed political work of creating social and economic
policies that bend history toward justice and equity instead of continuously
protecting the already affluent.

We have seen in this study that the current stratification of schools
reproduces inequality through a chartering process that includes credentialism and the formation of class consciousness. How would a grassroots
approach to educational policy address those two mechanisms for reproducing a class-based school system? We have learned that the formation of
collective memory is a very powerful means for reproducing inequality because class differences are internalized and therefore largely unquestioned.
Breaking the cycle of internalization will not be easy because it is structural
and forms a mental framework for most people.

I believe we need to tackle the challenge of freeing our school system
from reproducing inequality from four perspectives: revise our method of
funding public education, begin the process of creating trans-class curriculum and learning opportunities in order to create shared American collective
memories, place education back into the hands of teachers and educators,
and curtail the current testing regime.

1. It is astounding to observers from other countries that we spend
   more on the education of affluent children than poor children. I
   have suggested elsewhere that we reallocate resources from our
   very large national defense budget to our public schools (Cookson,
   2011). I also suggest that we develop finance equity formulas
   that ensure that children in working-class and poor schools have
   enough money to feed their students, provide up-to-date books and
   technology, and have available the academic and human services
   students need.
2. Today, our curriculum is exclusionary and class-based. Educational
   visionaries such as James Banks (1997) at the University of
   Washington have developed multicultural curriculum; I suggest
   we develop *multiclass* curriculum, or more precisely, trans-class
   21st-century curriculum. This curriculum would go a long way
   toward breaking down the rigid divisions in children's educational

opportunities by beginning the process of creating interclass shared memories and a shared culture. As long as the privileged classes can maintain the mythology that their history is the real history, we will continue to have a dangerous stratification of knowledge that becomes a form of unearned cultural capital. This trans-class curriculum should include cross-school visitations, shared field trips (not just to art museums, but to those hidden places where inequality hides), and teacher exchanges in which all teachers have the opportunity to teach in schools that vary by the social class background of their students.

3. It is time to come to our senses and place education back into the hands of the only people who actually know how learning takes place and how good schools are run: teachers. Teachers are natural experimenters when given the chance. They have their ears to the educational ground and know the students. A grassroots reform perspective must begin with teachers.

4. Today's testing regime perpetuates class divisions. Supposedly based on merit, standardized tests are, in reality, tests of who is in possession of the most class-based cultural capital. Finland did not become the number-one school system in the world because it spent precious resources paying corporations huge amounts of money to concoct tests that are intellectually questionable.

Will these policy baby steps make a difference and move us down the road to educational excellence and equality of opportunity? Only time will tell. First steps should not be viewed as ends in themselves but as the first of a sequenced set of policies that are designed to liberate learning from the iron grip of class reproduction. Baby steps are important because this is how societies learn to walk on their own two feet. If we can succeed in taking the first tentative steps toward educational justice, we will soon be running in the direction of equality of educational opportunity.

DARE THE SCHOOL BUILD A NEW SOCIAL ORDER?

Schooling is at the center of our deepest social struggle. Leveling the educational playing field will not be easy because there is a powerful coalition of vested interests who have a large stake in keeping things the way they are. As we have seen in these pages, class is not only an objective reality, but it also makes up the fabric of our consciousness. Educational reproduction is a conveyer belt of pain for so many. Genuine liberation for all of us is to first recognize how much pain educational inequality causes and then to link arms to reframe and reconstruct a system of public schools where every child and young adult has a real opportunity to develop his or her talent. In order to transform the future, we need to regain faith in our collective life. We need to affirm the value of good government, the value of community, and the value of the genuine rights of individuals.

We ended the introduction of this book with a question that was first posed by George Counts in 1932: Dare the school build a new social order? Perhaps it is time to ask this question again. As we begin to think about unraveling the straitjacket that class relations have woven around our school system, we need to ask ourselves how we can interrupt the processes of class reproduction.

Schools can build a new social order because they are the nurseries of consciousness. There are those who think that to mention the development of a new social consciousness indicates a lack of realism. But consider this: "Realism" has brought us to the brink of an educational meltdown and as a consequence the United States is well on its way to losing its global leadership and taking its place as another historic also-ran. The world's most dynamic economies have embraced educational innovation with a vengeance, and it will not be long before we find ourselves living on borrowed money and being relegated to the sidelines of history. A new shared vision of an inclusive and innovative system of schools, serving all children, is the soundest investment we can make to ensure that our grand social experiment, begun with so much bravery and hope, does not, in Abraham Lincoln's words, perish from this earth.

Appendix:
School Portraiture with an Edge

In 1983 sociologist Sara Lawrence-Lightfoot published *The Good High School: Portraits of Character and Culture.* Her study fully captured Waller's (1932) concept of schools being little more than sites for interacting relationships. She drew sensitive and compelling portraits of six strikingly different schools, explaining her unique methodology as follows:

> I also wanted to enter into relationships with my "subjects" that had the quality of empathic regard, full and critical attention, and a discerning gaze. The encounters, fully developed, would allow me to reveal the underside, the rough edges, the dimensions that often go unrecognized in the subjects themselves. (Lawrence-Lightfoot, 1983, p. 6)

The notion that sociology should borrow from art was, and still is, revolutionary. The traditional sociological value is to stand outside looking in, so to speak. But often, this approach results in a cold and ultimately unrealistic portrait of schools. Like individuals, schools have an inner life that surveys can't capture. In Lawrence-Lightfoot's words (1983), "Artists must not view the subject as object, but as a person of myriad dimensions" (pp. 5–6). In writing about how portraiture can be applied to the sociological analysis of schools, she describes her work as follows:

> In the six portraits, I seek to capture the culture of the schools, their essential features, their generic character, the values that define their curriculum goals and institutional structures, and their individual styles and rituals. (p. 6)

It is this multidimensionality that I hoped to capture in my portraits of the schools in this study. I don't believe, however, that portraits should disguise the underlying reality of the sitter or the school. Good portraits don't cover up warts or airbrush away wrinkles or blemishes. Moreover, the artist needs a perspective. Portraits are most revealing when they see the sitter from a specific angle and light that reveals that which the sitter might wish to conceal. Although I deeply appreciate all the good things that can go on in high schools, I also recognize that if we stand back and examine them from the wider frame of their relation to society the picture is not always so pretty. My approach is to borrow from Lawrence-Lightfoot's insights but to keep the sociological edge sharp. Schools are not randomly organized or randomly scattered across the social landscape. They are expressions of the class structure.

In one sense, Lawrence-Lightfoot's approach is an ascetic expression of what anthropologists have been doing since the late 19th century. To understand a culture, the researcher needs to be open to novelty and train him- or herself to listen deeply and observe carefully. Understanding cultures requires a willingness to suspend judgment and an openness to surprise. Does it matter that schools that educate poor children run out of toilet paper regularly? Does it matter that the hallways of working-class and underclass schools continually echo with the sound of slamming doors during class time? Does it matter that students attending elite schools wear old loafers with no socks? Does it matter that the hallways and classrooms of middle-class high schools are decorated with posters of movie stars? Does it matter that many upper-middle-class students come to school in Mercedes and BMWs?

Looking at the cultural lives of schools prompts us to ask different questions than those that are normally found on state evaluations. Why, for instance, are students at the most elite schools apt to wear faux street clothing while impoverished students try their level best to look respectable? Why in the world do we insist that working-class kids line up for everything, while upper-class kids don't line up for anything other than the salad bar? Why are upper-middle-class kids afraid of making one academic mistake while they lead lives of careless sexuality and drug use? Why do private schools resist playing public schools at sports?

To the untrained observer, it might not seem as though these details are important, but to an experienced observer they speak volumes because they are the uncensored expressions of the school's cultural subtext. No one arrives at school saying, "Today, I am going to do everything in my power to reproduce the class system." People simply arrive and go about their lives, acting out their class ethos without much thought and few questions. That's why it works. Educational reproduction is the sum of a thousand small daily acts that students, teachers, and administrators take to be nothing more than the normal way of doing things. The cultural subtext is almost always left unquestioned.

Class reproduction is not a cookie-cutter process; it is acted out every day in ways that are playful, painful, paradoxical, and poignant. Students learn their class identity through a complex mixture of what they study, the educational philosophies of their teachers and principals, the social attitudes of other students, the attitudes of other students toward learning, the kinds of peer pressure exerted by socially dominant students, the image of future opportunities presented by the school, the presence or absence of a collective sense of efficacy and an inner locus of control, and the overall impact of the complex political, social, and cultural values associated with different classes.

Understanding this complexity takes a trained eye, open ears, and a mind that is willing to see things in a different light. Openness and suspension of judgment allows the researcher to see the "text" of the drama that is schooling, but also to see the subtext. What constitutes revealing data about the inner life of schools is by definition not subject to an Excel spreadsheet. I have found that purposeful observation, listening, and conversation are the best tools for gathering what might be thought of as *living* data. By studying schools from the inside out, by listening to the voices of real people, and by removing the blinders of social convention we can see that which is hidden in the numbers.

A complete picture of the class reproduction process, however, needs to transcend the telling details; it needs to weave these details into a coherent picture that tells a story with a strong plot and meaningful theme. Stories, to be convincing social science, must be woven into a larger picture. This is accomplished by connecting the seen and unseen forces that map the social terrain; the successful cartographer of class relations not only has a sociological compass, she or he is also equipped with theoretically tested social topographical maps and seismic social sensors.

Schools are the sum total of their messages—every school is a metaphor for the past, present, and the future. The messages students receive are complex and go far beyond official mission statements or the professed goals of the school. This messaging is essentially a 360-degree experience; if school walls could talk, they would tell the story of generations of students who, without knowing it, have internalized their school's deep curriculum. Powerful cultures create shared commonsense understandings that may seem real but are in fact myths dressed up as reality.

Capturing an all-embracing experience in linear and literal language is a challenge. How do you summarize the cumulative effects of a school's physical presence, its culture of teaching and learning, and a thousand other small but significant factors? For instance, why is shouting tolerated in working-class and underclass schools, but rarely in middle- and upper-class schools? Could it be that for the working poor and the poor, schools are extensions of the street, whereas schools that are preparing students for the world of white-collar work are extensions of the office?

Food is a deep socializer because whoever controls our somatic needs controls us. Why is it that schools in areas of concentrated poverty barely have enough food to feed their students and the quality is generally low, whereas in upper-middle- and upper-class schools food is plentiful and healthy? What messages do students draw from this? When a middle-class student breaks a rule or gets into a fight, are the police called to "investigate"? Rarely, if ever. Visit almost any working-class or underclass school and you are likely to see not only school security but also regular police officers—their guns on display.

If you are a poor student and you have to go to the bathroom at an undesignated time, you will find the bathroom door locked and a security officer will most likely escort you to the restroom. I have never visited an upper-class school or middle-class school where students' bodily needs are so closely supervised. Many schools in areas of concentrated poverty have airport-type security screen stations at the front door; I have never seen this in schools enrolling middle-, upper-middle-, and upper-class students. If the medium is the message, then it may not be an exaggeration to describe much of the education of the poor as the school-to-prison pipeline, and the education of the affluent as the school-to-boardroom pipeline.

References

Aldrich, N. W. Jr. (1988). *Old money: The mythology of wealth in America*. New York: Allworth Press.

Alexander, K. L., Fennessey, J., McDill, E. L., & D'Amico, R. J. (1979). School SES influences—composition or context? *Sociology of Education, 52,* 222–237.

Allan, K. D. (2010). *Explorations in classical sociological theory: Seeing the social world*. Thousand Oaks, CA: Pine Forge Press.

Anyon, J. (1980). Social class and the hidden curriculum of work. *Journal of Education, 162,* 67–92.

Anyon, J. (1981). Social class and school knowledge. *Curriculum Inquiry, 11,* 3–42.

Anyon, J. (2006). Social class, school knowledge, and hidden curriculum: Retheorizing reproduction. In L.Weiss, C. McCarthy, & G. Dimitriadis (Eds.), *Ideology, curriculum and the new sociology of education* (pp. 37–46). New York: Routledge.

Apple, M. W. (1995). *Education and power* (2nd ed.). New York: Routledge.

Apple, M. W. (2004). *Ideology and curriculum* (3rd ed.). New York: Routledge.

Archer, M. (1979). *The social origins of educational systems*. London: Sage.

Archer, M. (2000). *Being human: The problem of agency*. Cambridge, UK: Cambridge University Press.

Aronowitz, S. (2003). *How class works: Power and social movement*. New Haven, CT: Yale University Press.

Baltzell, E. D. (1958). *Philadelphia gentleman: The making of a national upper class*. Chicago: Quadrangle Books.

Baltzell, E. D. (1964). *The Protestant establishment*. New York: Random House.

Bandura, A. (1993). Perceived self-efficacy in cognitive development and functioning. *Educational Psychologist, 28*(2), 117–148.

Banks, J. A. (1997). *Educating citizens in a multicultural society*. New York: Teachers College Press.

Bella, R. N. et. al. (1987). *Individualism and commitment in American life*. New York: Harper and Row.

Bigelow, W. (1992). Inside the classroom: social vision and critical pedagogy. In P. Shannon (Ed.), *Becoming political: Readings and writings in the politics of literacy education* (pp. 72–82). Portsmouth, NH: Heinemann.

Birmingham, S. (1987). *America's secret aristocracy*. Boston, MA: Little, Brown and Company.

Birnbach, L., with Kidd, C. (2010). *True prep: It's a whole new old world.* New York: Alfred A. Knopf.

Bloom, H. (2000). *Global brain: The evolution of mass mind from the big bang to the 21st century.* New York: John Wiley & Sons.

Bourdieu, P. (1984). *Distinction.* Cambridge, MA: Harvard University Press.

Bourdieu, P., & Passeron, J.-C. (1970). *Reproduction: In education, society, and culture.* Beverly Hills, CA: Sage.

Bowles, S., & Gintis, H. (1976). *Schooling in capitalist America.* New York: Basic Books.

Brantlinger, E. A. (1993a). *The politics of social class in secondary schools: Views of affluent and impoverished youth.* New York: Teachers College Press.

Brantlinger, E. A. (1993b). Adolescent's interpretation of social class influences on schooling. *Journal of Classroom Interaction, 28*(1), 1–12.

Brooks, D. (2000). *Bobos in paradise: The new upper class and how they got there.* New York: Simon & Schuster.

Centers, R. (1949). *The psychology of social class: A study of social classes.* Princeton, NJ: Princeton University Press.

Chubb, J. E., & Moe, T. M. (1990). *Politics, markets and America's schools.* Washington, DC: Brookings Institution.

Coleman, J. S. (1961). *The adolescent society: The social life of the teenager and its impact on education.* New York: Free Press.

Coleman, J. S., Campbell, E. Q., Hobson, C. J., McPartland, J., Wood, A. M., Weinfeld, F. D., & York, R. L. (1966). *Equality of educational opportunity.* Washington, DC: Office of Education, U.S. Department of Health, Education and Welfare, U.S. Government Printing Office.

Coleman, J. S., Hoffer, T., & Kilgore, S. (1981). *Public and private schools.* Chicago: National Opinion Research Center.

Collins, R. (1971). Functional and conflict theories of educational stratification. *American Sociological Review, 36,* 1002–1019.

Collins, R. (1975). *Conflict sociology: Toward an explanatory science.* New York: Academic Press.

Collins, R. (1979). *The credential society.* New York: Academic Press.

Connell, R. W., Ashenden, D., Kessler, S., & Dowsett, G. (1982, 2012). *Making a difference: Schools, families and social division.* North Sydney, Australia: Allen & Unwin.

Cookson, P. W. Jr. (1981). Private secondary boarding schools and public suburban high school graduation: An analysis of college attendance plans. Ph.D. dissertation, New York University.

Cookson, P. W. Jr. (1994). *School choice: The struggle for the soul of American education.* New Haven, CT: Yale University Press.

Cookson, P. W. Jr. (2009a). Perspectives on elite boarding schools. *Handbook of research on school choice.* New York: Routledge.

Cookson, P. W. Jr. (2009b). American boarding schools. *Chicago companion to the child*. Chicago, IL: University of Chicago Press.

Cookson, P. W. Jr. (2010). The religious origins of American boarding schools. *The encyclopedia of religion in America*. Washington, DC: Congressional Quarterly Press.

Cookson, P. W. Jr. (2011). *Sacred trust: A children's education bill of rights*. Thousand Oaks, CA: Corwin Press.

Cookson, P. W. Jr., & Embree, K. (1999). The Edison partnership schools: An assessment of academic climate and classroom culture. *The National Education Association*. Retrieved from www.nea.org/issues/corpmngt.cookrpt.htm

Cookson, P. W. Jr., & Persell, C. H. (1985). *Preparing for power: America's elite boarding schools*. New York: Basic Books.

Cookson, P. W. Jr., & Persell, C. H. (1991). Race and class in America's elite boarding preparatory schools: African Americans as the "outsiders within." *The Journal of Negro Education, 60*(2), 219–228.

Cookson, P. W. Jr., & Persell, C. H. (2010). Preparing for power: twenty-five years later. In A. Howard & R. Gaztambide-Fernandez (Eds.), *Educating elites: Class, privilege, and educational advantage* (pp. 13–30). Lanham, MD: Rowman and Littlefield Education.

Counts, G. (1932). *Dare the school build a new social order?* New York: John Day Publishing.

Cremin, L. A. (1957). *The republic and the school: Horace Mann and the education of free men*. New York: Teachers College Press.

Csikszentmihalyi, M., & Larson, R. (1984). *Being adolescent: Conflict and growth in the teenage years*. New York: Basic Books.

Delpit, L. D. (2006). *Other people's children: Cultural conflict in the classroom*. New York: The New Press.

Demerath, P. (2009). *Producing success: The culture of personal advancement in an American high school*. Chicago: The University of Chicago Press.

DeParle, J. (2012, January 5). Harder for Americans to rise from lower rungs. *New York Times*. Retrieved from http://query.nytimes.com/gst/fullpage. html?res=9C07E5D61E3FF936A35752C0A9649D8B63&ref=jasondeparle

DiMaggio, P. (1982). Cultural capital and school success: The impact of status culture participation on the grades of US high school students. *American Sociological Review, 47*, 189–201.

Dornbush, S. M. (1955). The military academy as an assimilating institution. *Social Forces, 33*, 316–321.

Douthat, R. G. (2005). *Privilege: Harvard and the education of the ruling class*. New York: Hyperion.

Dovidio, J. F., Gaertner, S. L., & Saguy, T. (2009). Commonality and complexity of "we": Social attitudes and social change. *Personality and Social Psychology Review, 13*(3), 3–20.

Dreeben, R. (1968). *On what is learned in school*. Reading, MA: Addison-Wesley.

Duncan, O. D., Featherman, D. L., & Duncan, B. (1972). *Socioeconomic background and achievements*. New York: Seminar Press.

Durkheim, E. (1956). *Education and sociology*. Trans. S. D. Fox. New York: Free Press.

Dyson, G. B. (1997). *Darwin among the machines: The evolution of global intelligence*. New York: Basic Books.

Economic Policy Institute. (2012). CEOs made 231 times more than workers did in 2011. Retrieved from http://www.epi.org/news/ceos-231-times-workers-2011/

Ehrenreich, B. (1990). *Fear of falling: The inner life of the middle class*. New York: HarperCollins.

Erikson, E. H. (1963). *Childhood and society*. New York: W. W. Norton.

Etzioni, A. (1975). *A comparative analysis of complex organizations: On power, involvement, and their correlates*. New York: Free Press.

Faux, J. (2006). *The global class war*. Hoboken, NJ: John Wiley & Sons.

Femia, J. V. (1975). Hegemony and consciousness in the thought of Antonio Gramsci. *Political Studies, 23*, 29–48.

Fine, M. (1992). The "public" on public schools: The social construction/constriction of moral communities. In L.Weis, M. Fine, & A. Lareau (Eds.), *Schooling and silenced "others": Race and class in schools*. Buffalo, NY: Graduate School of Education Publications, Buffalo Research Institute on Education for Teaching, SUNY Buffalo.

Finn, P. J. (2009). *Literacy with an attitude: Educating working-class children in their own self-interest* (2nd ed.). Albany, NY: SUNY Press.

Finn, P. J. (2012). Preparing for power in elite boarding schools and working-class schools. *Theory into Practice, 51*, 57–63.

Flanagan, C. A., & Campbell, B. (2003). Social class and adolescents' beliefs about justice in different social orders. *Journal of Social Issues, 59*(4), 711–732.

Floud, J. E. (1973). *Social class and educational opportunity*. Westport, CT: Greenwood Press.

Frank, R. H., & Cook, P. J. (1995). *The winner-take-all society*. New York: Martin Kessler Books.

Freire, P. (1970). *Pedagogy of the oppressed*. New York: Seabury Press.

Friedman, M. (1962). *Capitalism and freedom*. Chicago: University of Chicago Press.

Friedman, T. (2007). *The world is flat 3.0: A brief history of the 21st century*. New York: Picador.

Fussell, P. (1992). *Class: A guide through the American status system*. New York: Touchstone.

Giddens, A. (1973). *The class structure of advanced societies*. New York: Harper and Row.

Gilbert, D. (2011). *The American class structure in an age of growing inequality* (8th ed.). Thousand Oaks, CA: Pine Forge Press.

Goffman, E. (1959). *The presentation of self in everyday life.* New York: Doubleday.

Goffman, E. (1961). Symbols of class status. *British Journal of Sociology, 2,* 294–310.

Golden, D. (2007). *The price of admissions: How America's ruling class buys its way into elite colleges and who gets left outside the gates.* New York: Three Rivers Press.

Goode, W. J. (1967). The protection of the inept. *American Sociological Review, 32,* 5–19.

Goodman, E., Amick, B. C., Rezendes, M. O., Levine, S., Kagan, J., Rogers, W. H., & Talov, A. R. (2000). Adolescents' understanding of social class: A comparison of white upper middle class and working class youth. *Journal of Adolescent Health, 27,* 80–83.

Halsey, A. H., Heath, A. F., & Ridge, J. M. (1980). *Origins and destinations: Family, class and education in modern Britain.* Oxford, UK: Clarendon Press.

Halwachs, M. (1959). *The psychology of social class.* Glencoe, IL: Free Press.

Havinghurst, R. J., & Taba, H. (1949). *Adolescent character and personality.* Oxford, UK: Wiley.

Heyns, B. (1974). Social selection and stratification within schools. *American Journal of Education, 79,* 1434–1451.

Hollingshead, A. B. (1949). *Elmstown's youth: The impact of social class on adolescents.* Oxford, UK: Wiley.

Hopper, E. (1971). Stratification, education and mobility in industrialized societies. In E. Hopper (Ed.), *Readings in the theory of educational systems* (pp. 13–37). London: Hutchinson.

Hummelweit, H. T., Halsey, A. H., & Oppenheim, A. N. (1952). The views of adolescents on some aspects of the social class structure. *The British Journal of Sociology, 3* (2), 148–172.

Institute for Children, Poverty & Homelessness. (2011). *On the brink: Homelessness a reality in the South Bronx.* New York: Author.

Iscol, J., & Cookson, P. W. Jr. (2011). *Hearts on fire: Twelve stories of today's visionaries igniting idealism into action.* New York: Hummingbird Projects.

Jencks, C. J., & Brown, M. D. (1975). Effects of high schools on their students. *Harvard Educational Review, 45,* 273–324.

Jencks, C. J., Smith, M., Acland, H., Bane, M. J., Cohen, D., Gintis, H., Heyns, B., & Michelson, S. (1972). *Inequality.* New York: Basic Books.

Judge, T. A., & Bono, J. E. (2001). Relationship of core self-evaluations traits—self-esteem, generalized self-efficacy, locus of control, emotional stability—with job satisfaction and job performance: A meta-analysis. *Journal of Applied Psychology, 86*(1), 80–92.

Kalhenberg, R. D. (2000). *A notion at risk: Preserving public education as an engine for social mobility.* Washington, DC: The Century Fund.

Kalhenberg, R. D. (2001). *All together now: Creating middle-class schools through public school choice.* Washington, DC: Brookings Institution Press.

Kamens, D. (1977). Legitimating myths and educational organization: The relationship between organizational ideology and formal structure. *American Sociological Review, 42,* 208–219.

Kania, J., & Kramer, M. (2011, Winter). Collective impact. *Stanford Social Innovation Review.* Retrieved from http://www.ssireview.org/articles/entry/collective_impact

Kawachi, I., Kennedy, B. P., Lochner, K., & Prothrow-Stith, D. (1997). Social capital, income inequality, and mortality. *American Journal of Public Health, 87*(9), 1491–1498.

Kerckhoff, A. C. (1972). *Socialization and social class.* Englewood Cliffs, NJ: Prentice-Hall.

Kett, J. F. (1977). *Rites of passage: Adolescence in America 1790 to the present.* New York: Basic Books.

Kingston, P. (2001). *The classless society.* Palo Alto, CA: Stanford University Press.

Kohn, M. L. (1969). *Class and conformity: A study in values.* Homewood, IL: Dorsey.

Kohn, M. L. (1976). Class and parental values: another conformation of the relationship. *American Sociological Review, 41,* 538–545.

Kohn, M. L., & Schooler, C. (1983). *Work and personality: An inquiry into the impact of social stratification.* Norwood, NJ: Ablex.

Kozol, J. (1991). *Savage inequalities: Children in America's schools.* New York: Crown Publishing.

Lakoff, G. (2004). *Don't think of an elephant: Know your values and frame the debate.* White River Junction, VT: Chelsea Green Publishing.

Lapham, L. H. (1988). *Money and class in America.* London, UK: Weidenfeld & Nicholson.

Lareau, A. (2003). *Unequal childhoods: Class, race and family life.* Berkeley, CA: University of California Press.

Lareau, A., & Conley, D. (2008). *Social class.* New York: Russell Sage.

Lawrence-Lightfoot, S. (1983). *The good high school: Portraits of character and culture.* New York: Basic Books.

Leahy, R. L. (1981). The development of the conception of economic inequality. *Child Development, 52,* 523–532.

Leahy, R. L. (1983a). Development of the conception of economic inequality: explanations, justifications, and concepts of social mobility and change. *Development Psychology, 19*(1), 111–125.

Leahy, R. L. (1983b). *The child's construction of social inequality.* New York: Academic Press.

LeDoux, J. E. (2003). *The synaptic self: How our brains become who we are.* New York: Penguin Group.

Lenski, G. E. (1966). *Power and privilege: A theory of social stratification.* New York: McGraw-Hill.

Levine, S. B. (1980). Private education and class integration. *Social Problems, 28*, 63–94.

Lewis, L. S., & Wanner, R. A. (1979). Private schooling and the status attainment process. *Sociology of Education, 52*, 99–112.

Loftus, E. (1980). *Memory: Surprising new insights into how we remember and why we forget.* Reading, MA: Addison-Wesley.

Lucas, S. R. (1999). *Tracking inequality: Stratification and mobility in American high schools.* New York: Teachers College Press.

MacLeod, J. (1987). *Ain't no making it: Aspiration and attainment in a low-income neighborhood.* Boulder, CO: Westview Press.

McDill, E. L., & Rigsby, L. C. (1973). *Structure and process in secondary schools: The academic impact of academic climates.* Baltimore, MD: Johns Hopkins University Press.

Metz, M. (2003). *Different by design: The context and character of three magnet schools.* New York: Sociology of Education Series.

Meyer, J. W. (1970). The charter: Conditions of diffuse socialization in schools. In W. R. Scott (Ed.), *Social processes and social structure* (pp. 564–578). New York: Holt, Rinehart & Winston.

Meyer, J. W. (1972). The effects of institutionalization on colleges in society. In K. A. Feldman (Ed.), *College and student: Selected readings in the social psychology of higher education* (pp. 109–126). New York: Pergamon Press.

Meyer, J. W. (1977). The effects of education as an institution. *American Journal of Sociology, 83*, 55–77.

Miller, D. L. (1982). *The individual and the social self: Unpublished work of George Herbert Mead.* Chicago: University of Chicago Press.

Mills, C. W. (1956). *The power elite.* London: Oxford University Press.

Morgan, G. (1986). *Images of organization.* Beverly Hills, CA: Sage.

Morrison, T. (2011). Commencement address Rutgers University. Retrieved from http://llanoralleyne.com/2011/05/toni-morrisons-commencement-address-to-rutgers-university-class-of-2011/

Murray, M. (2004). *Freaks, geeks and cool kids: American teenagers, schools, and the culture of consumption.* New York: Routledge.

Oakes, J. (2005). *Keeping track: How schools structure inequality.* New Haven, CT: Yale University Press.

Oakes, J., & Rogers, J. (2006). *Learning power: Organizing for education and justice.* New York: Teachers College Press.

Olson, M. Jr. (1965). *The logic of collective action: Public goods and the theory of groups.* Cambridge, MA: Harvard University Press.

Organization for Economic Co-Operation and Development. (2010). *Economic survey of Finland 2010.* Retrieved from http://www.oecd.org/eco/economicsurveyoffinland2010.htm

Ornstein, A. C. (2007). *Class counts: Education, inequality and the shrinking middle class.* Lanham, MD: Rowan & Littlefield.

Parenti, M. (1988). *Democracy for the few.* New York: St. Martin's Press.

Parkin, F. (1971). *Class, inequality & political order.* New York: Praeger.

Parkin, F. (1974). *Social analysis of class structure.* London: Tavistock Press.

Parsons, T. (1968). The school class as a social system. *Harvard Educational Review Reprint, 1,* 69–90.

Persell, C. H. (1977). *Education and inequality.* New York: Free Press.

Powell, A. G., Farrar, E., & Cohen, D. K. (1985). *The shopping mall high school.* Boston: Houghton Mifflin.

Pratto, F., Sidanius, J., Stallworth, L. M., & Malle, B. F. (1994). Social dominance orientation: A personality variable predicting social and political attitudes. *Journal of Personality and Social Psychology, 67*(4), 741–763.

Ravitch, D. (2010). *The life and death of the great American school system: How testing and choice are undermining education.* New York: Basic Books.

Rehberg, R. A., & Rosenthal, E. R. (1978). *Class and merit in the American high school: An assessment of revisionist and meritocratic arguments.* New York: Longman.

Riihela, M., Sullstrom, R., Suoniemi, L., & Tuomala, M. (2002). *Recent trends in income inequality in Finland.* Helsinki, Finland: Labour Institute for Economic Research, Discussion Paper 183.

Robinson, R. V. (1984). Reproducing class relations in industrial capitalism. *American Sociological Review, 49,* 182–196.

Rorty, R. (1989). *Contingency, irony, and solidarity.* Cambridge, UK: Cambridge University Press.

Rosenbaum, J. E. (1976). *Making inequality.* New York: Wiley.

Rosenberg, M., & Pearlin, L. I. (1978). Social class and self-esteem among children and adults. *American Journal of Sociology, 84*(1), 53–77.

Rossides, D. W. (1976). *The American class system.* Boston: Houghton Mifflin.

Rothenberg, P. S. (2000). *Invisible privilege: A memoir about race, class and gender.* Lawrence: The University of Kansas Press.

Rothkopf, D. (2008). *Superclass: The global power elite and the world they are making.* New York: Farrar, Straus, & Giroux.

Rothstein, R. (2004). *Class and schools: Using social, economic, and educational reform to close the Black-White achievement gap.* New York: Teachers College Press.

Roy, J. (2005). Low income hinders college attendance for even the highest achieving students. Retrieved from www. EPI.org

Rutter, M., Maughan, B., Mortimore, P., Ouston, J., & Smith, A. (1979). *Fifteen thousand hours: Secondary schools and their effects on children.* Cambridge, MA: Harvard University Press.

Ryan, J. E. (2010). *Five miles away, a world apart: One city, two schools and the story of educational opportunity in modern America.* New York: Oxford University Press.

Sacks, P. (2007). *Tearing down the gates: Confronting the class divide in American education*. Berkeley, CA: University of California Press.

Sadovnik, A. R. (2001, December). Basil Bernstein 1924–2000. *Prospects: The quarterly review of comparative education, XXXI*(4), 678–703.

Sahlberg, P. (2011). *Finnish lessons: What can the world learn from educational change in Finland?* New York: Teachers College Press.

Sennett, R., & Cobb, J. (1972). *The hidden injuries of class*. New York: Knopf. [Reissued by Yale University Press, 2008]

Simmons, R. G., & Rosenberg, M. (1971). Functions of children's perceptions of the stratification system. *American Sociological Review, 36,* 235–249.

Small, M. F. (1990, March/April). Political animals: Social intelligence and the growth of the primate brain. *The Sciences,* 36–42.

Stendler, C. B. (1949). *Children of Brasstown: Their awareness of the symbols of social class*. Urbana: University of Illinois Press.

Tavernise, S. (2012, February 9). Education gap grows between rich and poor, studies say. *New York Times*. Retrieved from http://www.nytimes.com/2012/02/10/education/education-gap-grows-betweenrichandpoorstudiesshow.html?pagewanted=all&_r=0&gwh=CC38B998B896C487D20D041C13D1B6CC

Tumin, M. M. (1953). Some principles of stratification: A critical analysis. *American Sociological Review, 18*(4), 387–393.

Turner, R. H. (1960). Sponsored and contest mobility and the school system. *American Sociological Review, 25,* 855–862.

Tutor, J. (1991). The development of class awareness in children. *Social Forces, 49,* 470–476.

Waller, W. (1932). *The sociology of teaching*. New York: Wiley.

Weis, L. (1990). *Working class without work: High school students in a de-industrializing economy*. New York: Routledge.

Wexler, P., Crichlow, W., Kern, J., & Matusewicz, R. (1992). *Becoming somebody: Toward a social psychology of school*. Abingdon, UK: RoutledgeFalmer.

Willis, P. (1977). *Learning to labour: How working class kids get working class jobs*. New York: Columbia University Press.

Winters, J. A. (2011, November–December). Democracy and oligarchy. *The American Interest, VII*(2), 18–27.

Wright, E. O. (2008). Logics of class analysis. In A. Lareau & D. Conley (Eds.), *Social Class* (pp. 329–349). New York: Russell Sage.

Wrong, D. H. (1979). *Power: Its forms, bases, and uses*. New York: Harper Colophon.

Index

Achievement/Achievement gap. *See* Student achievement

Aciand, H., vii, 2

Adolescence
   characteristics of, 27
   class rite of passage in, baptismal analogy for, 30
   defined, 27

Adolescent socialization, 28–30
   social class and, 23–24

Adolescents' Understanding of Social Class (Goodman et al.), 23–24

Advantaged/disadvantaged students
   cumulative social process and, 15
   legitimizing cultural achievements of, 15

Agency, acquiring sense of, 38–39

Agency, social structure and, 2. *See also* Socialization

Aldrich, N. W. Jr., 8

Alexander, K. L., 7

Allan, K. D., 2

Allocation. *See* Role allocation

Althusser, L., 30

American Community Survey (2010), ix

Amick, B. C., 23–24

Anyon, J., vii, 89

Apple, M. W., 1, 37

Archer, M., 1, 2

Architectural/Ascetic narrative, 37
   at Highridge Academy (upper-class private school), 45–46

at Meadowbrook High (upper-middle-class suburban public high school), 58–60

at Patrick Henry High (working-class rural public high school), 82–84

at Riverside High (middle-class neighborhood public high school), 71–73

at Roosevelt High (impoverished inner-city neighborhood public high school), 96–98

Aronowitz, S., 8, 55

Ashenden, D., 1

Assimilation, identity and, 29

Aud, S., viii, ix

Authority narrative, 37
   at Highridge Academy (upper-class private school), 46–48
   at Meadowbrook High (upper-middle-class suburban public high school), 60–61
   at Patrick Henry High (working-class rural public high school), 84–86
   at Riverside High (middle-class neighborhood public high school), 73–74
   at Roosevelt High (impoverished inner-city neighborhood public high school), 98–99

Awareness, of class. *See* Class consciousness

About the Author

Peter W. Cookson Jr. is a prolific writer and sociologist. He is the author or coauthor of more than 15 books on education reform and policy. Currently, he is managing director and a senior fellow with Education Sector in Washington, D.C., and teaches at Teachers College (Columbia University) and Georgetown University. He is president of Ideas without Borders, an educational consulting firm specializing in 21st-century education, technology, and human rights. He blogs regularly for the *Huffington Post* and *Education Sector*.